Translucent Databases

Peter Wayner

Flyzone Press
Baltimore

Programming computers, designing databases and building secure networks is not a simple job. This book contains source code for some examples. While every effort is made to ensure that the source code is correct, neither the publisher nor the author can offer any warranty for its suitability, accuracy, quality, or completeness. If you choose to use any of the software or algorithms in this book, please work with a professional cryptographer, database administrator, or computer security expert. If you choose to apply the software to medical records or other applications in the world of health care, please check with the U.S. Food and Drug Administration. Some applications require approval by regulatory bodies. None of the examples in this book were scrutinized by these regulators. If you choose to use them for anything beyond illustration, please consult with recognized professionals who can guide you through the regulations. Neither the author nor the publisher offers any WARRANTY, either written or implied, for the software, algorithms or descriptions.

Flyzone Press
PO Box 5609
Baltimore, MD 21210
World Wide Web site at http://www.flyzone.com

An Imprint of Flyzone S.R. LLC

Wayner, Peter, 1964–
        Translucent Databases / Peter Wayner.
            p.   cm.
        Includes index.
        ISBN 0-12-738671-8 (alk. paper)
        1. Computer networks—Security measures.   2. Cryptography.   3. Internet
    (Computer networks)   I. Title.

Printed in the United States of America
02   03   04   05   06

Contents

Preface

Databases are valuable tools. Cryptography is a fascinating science. To date, the two mix in only the most basic ways. This book tries to outline some better techniques for mixing the two areas and creating better, faster, and more secure databases.

The book is designed to be practical. The equations are kept to a minimum, and usable Java code is added to the text. The chapters concentrate on exploring the ideas at a high level. If you're going to use these ideas on a regular basis in full-scale production environments, then you might consider reading some of the other books described in the Further Reading section. (Appendix A) These details can be very important in some contexts.

If you have any questions, suggestions or bug reports, please write to me. I will pay $5 to the first person to report each technical error. Watch the website (`http://www.wayner.org/books/td/`) for corrections.[1]

Many of the corrections that are already incorporated in the book are due to the suggestions of people who read early copies of the manuscript. I would personally like to thank David Banisar, Jeff Bates, and Michael Widenius who offered many suggestions. Karen Freeman copy edited the book and fixed many problems with grammar, punctuation and spelling. I must also thank Caroline who fixed so many things.

Peter Wayner
Baltimore, MD
March 2002
p3@wayner.org
http://www.wayner.org

---

[1] I reserve the right to pay multiple awards in cases when several people submit the same error around the same time. The restriction exists to prevent everyone from demanding $5 per error. I also reserve the right to decide the size and extent of a technical error.

Chapter 1

Translucency

In the beginning, there was the file. Programmers with data to store designed their own structures and poured the numbers into the file. The computer's operating system kept it together in one big block. The programmer took care of the details.

In time, smart programmers began building abstract data manipulation engines to categorize, collate and tabulate the bits. These databases sprouted sophisticated features for chopping, slicing, sorting and repacking the information to suit their users' needs. Programmers began to move away from the data itself and began writing tools that told the database software what to do. That extra layer brought freedom, device independence and simplicity to the field.

When computers and users proliferated, the database creators found ways to let many people use the information at the same time. The databases became arbiters of access, ensuring that the data would remain pure and correct even when hundreds sent their changes, tweaks and revisions in at the same time. The software juggled the responses while making sure that the numbers continued to add up correctly.

In time, the need to handle more users and important data brought security challenges. Sensitive information like salaries or health records needed to be kept in one central database, but it couldn't be left in the open to be seen by everyone. The database creators added new features for ensuring that people saw only the information they were entitled to see. Some tables full of numbers could be seen by one group and some could be seen by another group. The database software sat in the middle as the referee. The data came and went whenever the database said it was okay. The information lived inside a safe fortress that made decisions. The database became a carefully guarded palace where the information lived like a royal family.

That is a wonderful arrangement in many ways. The best databases come with strong, well-tested security mechanisms that provide good protection for the information. The procedures are sophisticated and flexible so it is fairly easy to make sure that only the right information comes squirting out the door of the palace.

That approach isn't perfect. If someone manages to sneak in the backdoor of the palace, the attacker can see all the information with complete freedom. If someone discovers the right combination of passwords, that person owns the database and all the information in it.

Locking out the wrong people can be difficult. While the database designers may make the access mechanisms as elegant and seamless as possible, they can never eliminate the inherent complexity. Remembering passwords, juggling encryption keys and organizing connections is not a simple task. People make mistakes. Buttons are pushed at the wrong time. Files collect typos. Voilà. Someone is coming in the window.

Sometimes the dangers come from within. If one of the system administrators responsible for protecting the database turns traitor, all of the data is in trouble. Locking all of the information up in a fortress means trusting the walls and the people who guard the walls.

This book takes a different approach. Instead of leaving the data to pace the floors of the fortress unprotected, it describes solutions for encasing each number, word, phrase or bit in an individual suit of armor. Even if the walls tumble, the data is still protected. Even if the guards betray their orders, the information is still safe from the wrong eyes.

At first glance, this idea seems self-defeating. Adding layers of encryption around the data makes it impossible for everyone to see the data even those with legitimate needs. If the information is locked up in armor, how can the database provide the right answer to questions? How can the database deliver the correct values for salaries, drug prescriptions, criminal records or whatever the request seeks if the information is locked away? Someone needs a key to the trapdoor that slips through the layers of stone and metal. Someone has to have access, or the database is just a pile of broken bits.

Mihir Bellare and Ronald Rivest used the term "translucent" in a different way to describe an escrow system that allows the government probabilistic access to encrypted communications. [BR99]

This simple view is only half-true. In some cases, there's no substitute for complete access to the information. You can't write a check to someone if you don't know the person's salary. No worker would want to build a database that prevented check creation. But there are ways to design the database so it will let out some information while keeping crucial information private and secure. It is possible, for instance, to maintain a database that provides basic information about the average salary of the workers without keeping individual information about each person.

This book describes how to build databases that both keep information secure *and* accomplish useful tasks. The algorithms use encryption to lock up the data in such a way that it still falls in a useful pattern. People can access the right information, but they cannot see what they aren't entitled to view. The artful use of encryption guarantees that the data is still secure if the palace walls are breached.

These solutions will be called *translucent databases* because they let some light escape the system while still providing a layer of secrecy. The notion of a translucent database is more a vision and a goal than a well-defined predicate. Here are some of the features that are part of the vision:

Encryption Translucent databases keep the data secure with one-way functions and encryption.

Ignorance In many cases, the data is scrambled by the user's computer before it travels over the network. The translucent database never sees the real information hidden inside.

Minimization Translucent databases obscure information by keeping the minimum amount of data necessary. If the ZIP code or other postal code suffices, there's no need to store the entire address.

Misdirection Some translucent databases add fake data into the mix. Only the legitimate user can spot the real items. Everyone else is locked out. That can be quite useful if no encryption is permitted. Mixing in spurious data can be just as good.

Stunt Data Translucent databases can replace data with encrypted items that can protect the real data while still looking like the real information. Such stunt data still obeys the right mathematical rules, but it protects the real information from revelation.

Equivalence Sometimes translucent databases obscure sensitive information by replacing it with a similar value that is functionally equivalent. There may be no reason to keep a person's full height when it's possible to replace these values with "tall", "average" or "short".

Quantization Reducing the precision of numbers or values can add privacy and security without destroying usability. There may be no need to keep all information with complete precision when keeping only the first couple of digits suffices. The latitude and longitude of a location can be recorded in degrees alone while obscuring the minutes and seconds.

This is not a solid definition, and not every translucent database uses every possible feature. Some merely minimize the data. Others use complicated layers of encryption to lock up the information and provide strange levels of access. Some mix and match a number of techniques. All of them adhere to the book's basic theme that databases don't need to have access to all of the information to accomplish their goals.

In essence, translucent databases are more like neutral switches for data than like all-seeing, omnipotent overlords of information. They move information without seeing crucial bits. They rely on intelligent clients on the edge of the network to bundle much of the information. They reduce complexity and responsiblity by knowing less and seeing little.

Reducing the amount of useful information in one central location offers a number of distinct advantages:

Security Translucent databases offer more security. Even if invaders find all of the passwords to all of the levels, they still won't get at the personal information. The raw data stored in the database is scrambled so that no one can see it, even if the attacker ties up the database administrator and tortures some small children.

OS Independence Even the best databases need to rely on the OS for security. If someone can sneak past the OS, the attacker can even read the information in the files. If the files are scrambled in a proprietary format, a clever hacker can still grab them when they're unscrambled in memory. All of the major operating systems are insecure. Patching all of the holes is a full-time job. Translucent databases protect the information even when the OS is compromised because translucent databases don't need to see the naked data.

Privacy Centralized information can be dangerous in the wrong hands. Many institutions continue to stand helpless as the clerks, managers or corporate bosses entrusted with caring for the data betray them. There are countless stories about workers everywhere who realize that the data at their fingertips is very valuable. Hospital clerks use Social Security numbers to get credit cards in other people's names. Motor vehicle clerks create fake licenses in other people's names. Translucent databases protect privacy by accomplishing their goals without keeping the naked information.

Freedom Many people keep complete records out of sheer habit. Writing everything down and storing it is a sensible way to prepare for a rainy day. This information, however, is also a responsibility. Many companies maintain a full-time staff to respond to subpoenas. FedEx, for instance, is constantly asked for shipping records. Divorce lawyers love to subpoena the toll booth data from drivers who use automated payment mechanisms. Translucent databases reduce the amount of visible data and provide freedom from requests.

Simplicity Translucent databases concentrate on delivering answers, not enforcing security rules. If all of the information is kept behind the impenetrable wall of encryption, then it doesn't matter who sees it. This means that the database can be simpler, smaller, and faster. The database does not need to search for the answer while simultaneously making sure that the request comes from someone with the correct authorization.

Mixed Access Translucent databases can give different people different results. One example in the book (Chapter 9) tracks Navy ships. A member of the public gets basic details about a ship's location while the admirals can use a special password to pinpoint the ship's position precisely. Mixing the different information into one database is simpler to administer.

Speed The simplicity translates into faster searches. Every level can be tuned to answering questions, not enforcing a complicated security model.

More information can be stored in RAM, and fewer operations need to be done to release it.

Distributed Workload Some of these claims of speed and simplicity are a bit disingenuous. Translucent databases still need encrypted data, but in many cases this work is done on the user's computer, not on the central machine. These local machines are often underutilized, and extra encryption costs little. Making better use of the user's machine also increases security. Data does not travel on the network unprotected. Once it leaves the user's machine, it's locked up for good. The database doesn't try to unscramble it.

Lower Costs Simpler databases can on run simpler and thus, less costly machines. The same job can be done with less RAM in less time on fewer processors.

Flexibility Ordinary databases require a sophisticated support crew to maintain them and provide ample security. Translucent databases may still require the services of good database administrators, but they can live on simpler, less guarded machines. It might make sense to locate a local copy of a database at a branch office. Translucent databases can protect the local information without a sophisticated security team. Simpler machines require less care.

All of these advantages are not absolute. Translucent databases may be simpler in some senses, but they are more complex in others. The basic database does not need to support complicated access systems, but the overall system does need to provide it. The work is just shifted from one layer to another. That can still provide substantial benefits, but they are not guaranteed to be free from headaches.

In some cases, the advantages are overwhelmed by the limitations. There are some cases where you really need to see the data. The value of having the data available in an emergency outweighs the value gained by using a simpler translucent system. These instances are often rarer than it might first appear. Many problems can be solved with a translucent database if a few changes are made. Sometimes seeing the real true values of the data is not essential. In other cases, a secondary copy of the database with translucent data can be used for average requests. The complete database with all of the sensitive information can be locked up with very serious and cumbersome access protections.

1.1   Some Examples

Consider the database containing the launch codes for nuclear missiles. That data is both very valuable and very dangerous if it falls into the wrong hands.

Maintaining a database with these launch codes is feasible because the high value justifies the levels of security and protection.

Now, consider a database with the food requests of everyone in the White House including the president. The database might help the White House chef choose menus, but it would also be quite dangerous in the hands of an assassin with a bottle of poison. In such a situation, a translucent database can help the chef organize the cooking without storing personal information where it might fall into the wrong hands. Scrambling much of the personal information means there's less need to protect the database, and giving access to workers is simpler.

In the past, security concerns may have trumped the need for an acessible kitchen database. But providing the same security for the kitchen data as for the nuclear launch codes may be financially and practically impossible. Translucent databases offer a feasible compromise.

Many of the best examples of good uses for translucent databases can be found where the data is more valuable to malicious users than it is to legitimate ones. If the cost of a database security breach is larger than the value of having the database, many businesses might choose not to keep the database. Owners of translucent databases don't need to worry about ordinary security breaches, so they can be quite useful in these situations.

Here are some others:

Passwords One of the first and best examples of a translucent database is the UNIX password file, an approach which is now widely imitated. [MT79, FK89, Man96] The UNIX system scrambles each password with an irreversible mechanism. When someone logs in, the password typed is scrambled using the same mechanism. If the results match, then the password is correct. The mechanism's irreversible nature, however, prevents someone from taking the password file and using the information. It may be possible to do a brute-force search, but there are no known easier attacks. This technique is used frequently to store passwords, and some databases have built-in functions to handle it.

A translucent database lowers the cost of passwords so that any basic system can maintain the file in a relatively unprotected part of the file system. Effective security is still possible even to restrict legitimate users. If there were no such database, it might be impossible to build simple and effective multiuser systems because one user might be able to see the password of another.

Scheduling Sites Wouldn't it be nice to have a central site for synchronizing all of the schedules in your life? If you wanted a baby sitter for Friday night, you could find out who was free with one click instead of a dozen phone calls. Unfortunately, such centralized databases can be quite dangerous. A collection of schedules for baby sitters contains two sensitive lists: the schedules for teenagers and the names of parents who will

Chapter 5 examines synchronization techniques.

be away from the house. Thieves and rapists are just two major groups who might be interested in the data.

A translucent database with no personal information is an ideal solution to this problem. If no one can read the database, then no one can abuse it. However, the users who know the right passwords can still find ways to make appointments.

Databases of Shopping Habits Would you like to be able to reorder the same pair of pants or shoes with one click? Do you have the time to remember whether the Size 11 or the Size $11\frac{1}{2}$ shoes from one manufacturer fit your feet like a glove? These little tidbits of information don't offer much value to the customer in the grand scheme of things, but they can turn out to be a bit embarrassing. Some people don't want you to know that their waistbands have expanded a few inches every year. Some people don't want you to know that they have Size 13 feet.

None of that information is very valuable to either the consumer or the antagonist and so the application is an ideal use of a translucent database. The database contains all of the information that might be of use to a customer, but no one, including the clerks at the store, can browse and discover the true sizes of their neighbors. An ideal translucent database can still provide larger statistical information about the buyers to guide future orders for the store without revealing all of the personal information to the ordering department.

When all things are equal, translucence in writing is more effective than transparency, just as glow is more revealing than glare.
–James Thurber Memo to the New Yorker

Prescription Information Many people are quite sensitive about the drugs they take. Insurance companies and employers can discriminate against them with the information. In many cases, the health of key people can affect a company's health and perhaps its stock price. The injury report from professional teams is very important to gamblers.

For all of these reasons and more, prescription information can be dangerous if it falls into the wrong hands. A good pharmacist, though, must also guard against potentially dangerous drug interactions. Knowing what people are taking is important.

A translucent database can solve many of these problems by locking up the information in such a way that no one can browse the database looking for people taking antidepressants. The system is still not perfect because it must be able to identify the drug prescriptions when presented with a name, but it blocks random browsing.

In the interest of fairness, there are a number of places where translucent databases won't work. Sometimes the database is so valuable that extraordinary precautions can be taken to protect it. Sometimes the database has little value to anyone so there's no reason to protect the information.

Here are some cases like those:

Tax Records None of us would like the government to forget how much we paid them in tax. It would be depressing if there were no central repository with a list of who paid how much. It should be noted that we still need a backup system. People usually pay with a check to obtain a receipt for the taxes. Some even insist upon getting a return receipt for filing the forms. This parallel system of paper receipts acts as both a backup and a translucent, distributed database of who pays. It would be possible to do without the central database in many cases, although perhaps not all.

Light Bulb Replacement Records Do you want to know when the light bulbs in the street lamps were last replaced? This information might help the road crews plan ahead, but I have trouble imagining when it would be useful to anyone with malicious ends. Locking up this data in a translucent database would not affect everyday life, but it might make life difficult in some extraordinary occurrences. If the data isn't too valuable, there's no reason to protect it.

Pizza Delivery Records The driver needs to know which address ordered which kind of pizza. There's no way to use translucent techniques to keep this information secure without making it difficult, if not impossible, for the driver to match the pizzas to the people. Both bits of data must be kept unscrambled to accomplish the task.

The historical information is a different matter. A pizza manager may want to analyze complicated statistics about neighborhoods and ordering patterns to schedule workers and order ingredients. There is no real reason to know how many pizzas an individual house ordered. The manager is just after aggregates. Storing the historical information in a translucent database protects the privacy of the customers without compromising the ability to plan ahead.

There are many applications where the data itself is too valuable to lose, and these make poor choices for translucent databases. In some cases, the information might be stored in translucent databases later, when it is needed in different contexts.

The decision of whetehr to use a translucent database is also filled with some emotional calculus. One person may feel that the information is mission-critical while another might want to replace it with translucent data as soon as possible. Smart people arguing in good faith will still make different choices.

I will argue, though, that many applications are ideally suited for translucent databases, even those that might require transparency. Most of us have a packrat's instinct for saving bits of information *just in case* they're useful in the future. Many businesses keep voluminous records *just in case* some need comes along. Keeping transparent databases is an extension of this instinct of being prepared.

In many cases, translucent databases are ideal compromises for these records. If you're keeping the information around *just in case*, then you can often accept the limitations of a translucent database. The information does not have to be available every data, so it can be scrambled without much loss of effectiveness. If a need comes along, the translucent data can often suffice. That can provide an additional layer of security to customers and employees without failing to meet many of the potential needs that might arise.

1.2 Limits

The technology in this book is not perfect. The most secure database is one that immediately forgets everything stored into it. There's no danger that the grounding wire will ever reveal information to the wrong person.

Translucent databases are a compromise between complete transparency and complete opacity. They offer some forms of access while blocking others. In most cases, they block random browsing that might be useful to thieves, rapists, murderers or other criminals without restricting standard access. A pharmacy's computer might store customer records in a translucent database to protect customers. The systems can provide some secrecy because random browsing will not reveal who's taking antidepressants or AIDS medication. The databases must still be able to look up customers by name to protect them against potential drug interactions. This is still a weakness in the system. If you know a name, you can find out the person's records.

Other translucent approaches provide secrecy by aggregating the information of users. The database may store only the average value of a region. That can protect the individuals in most cases, but not if there are only a few people in the region. If there's only one person, then the database doesn't provide real protection by just storing the average.

There are many similar limitations. The scheduling algorithms in this book requires each user to provide *and remember* a password. If the user forgets, the information disappears. It can't be recovered.

The information is also vulnerable to other forms of attacks. The central database of a translucent system may be filled with scrambled data, but the individual computers on users' desks may still be vulnerable. Keyboard sniffing software and other tools can snag the information before it is scrambled and inserted into the translucent database.

Translucent databases are vulnerable to all of these attacks, including many of the other ones commonly found in the world of cryptography. Most of the algorithms used in this book fall under the heading of cryptography so it follows that the same weaknesses that affect general cryptographic software can also affect translucent systems.

The guiding principle of translucent databases, though, minimizes these weaknesses. Moving the sensitive information out of a central database means that any attackers will not have one-stop shopping. They must attack the computers of the users, not the central machine. The weaknesses are still there, but the effects are reduced dramatically.

1.3   How to Use the Book

This book bundles together many of the best techniques from the world of cryptography and statistics and repackages them as standard database solutions. Many of the results are presented as Java code that produces standard SQL.

None of the solutions in this book are new. Many come from the world of cryptography researcher where mathematicians are always examining strange formulas and discovering how they can be used to provide security. Users searching for deeper understanding should consult excellent reference books like *Applied Cryptography*[Sch95] or *Handbook of Applied Cryptography*.[MvV97] Both offer excellent surveys of the field along with greater attention to the potential dangers. More ambitious readers will want to read the original material, which is often found in the proceedings of conferences like *Crypto, EuroCrypt, AsiaCrypt,* and *Financial Cryptography*. Cryptography is a very subtle field where strange weaknesses appear in odd places. This book is not a treatment of the algorithms. While every effort is made to present useful techniques with simple language, it is not possible to offer all of the depth that is better explained in other sources.

The best way to use this book is to read each chapter and then imagine where the ideas might be used. Many of the solutions are not immediately obvious because of our packrat instincts. Try to think of how databases can be restructured to be as translucent as possible. You may not push actual databases to this limit, but it helps to understand just how far you might go.

Each chapter also includes simple working code. This is often far less complicated than real code, which must be both bulletproof and elegant. All of the examples were written to be as short as possible without excluding the essential point. In many cases, some of the extra functionality can offer other security. Please use these examples as illustrations, not guaranteed solutions.

1.4   Some Motivation

To close, here's an unordered list of stories reported in the news about security breaches and abuse of trust and authority. They make good case for translucent databases. Not all of them can be solved immediately with the techniques described in this book, but all of them show how the best traditional techniques are far from strong enough. Sometimes you need translucent solutions that lock away information from everyone including the most trusted.

- In July 2001, hackers discovered that the Commerce Department's Web site accidentally offered access to information about U.S. companies like their size, revenues, and trading partners in Europe. The data was collected with a pledge to keep it secret, but the backdoor let anyone view or modify the data. The site was, ironically, aimed at helping businesses protect the privacy of employees and customers. [McC01]

- A Congressional investigation in June 2000 revealed that the Federal Aviation Administration (FAA) did inadequate background checks on its contractors, giving foreign nationals access to the sensitive source code. [Lem00]

- A man wearing an Air Force major's uniform walked into an arsenal at Fort Meade, MD and left with 30 M-16s, 20 M-9s, and two Chevrolet Blazers. The man, who was not in the Air Force, also picked up 12,000 rounds of ammunition from another base in Pennsylvania. He told investigators that he "studied to be an officer through mail-order courses." His goal was to teach Civil Air Patrol cadets to shoot. He wasn't a member of the Civil Air Patrol either.[Vog00]

In the dark all men were the same color. In the dark our fellow man was seen more clearly than in the normal light of a New York night.
–Stephen Kennedy *Police Commissioner of NYC after the blackout in 1959*

- After the destruction of the World Trade Center, an investigation focused on which staff members approved the visas for the hijackers. One article noted that the staff members at the various embassies often didn't have access to the best information. "Congress's General Accounting Office reported in 1997 that some agencies were leery of plugging data into the system, fearing it could compromise their work and their secret sources." [CA01]

- The U.S. military uses the Social Security number as the serial number for soldiers. Prisoners of War disclosing this value give their captors access to bank accounts and other information.

- Users of Microsoft's Web server were shocked to discover that Microsoft engineers included a secret backdoor password to enter customers' sites. A spokesman said the act was approved and could lead to the firing of the programmer– if the person was ever discovered. [Bri00]

- A 35-year-old New York City man has been in and out of jail all of his adult life for infiltrating the transit system and masquerading as an employee. He told the New York Times in an interview from Riker's Island: "I am not insane; I am just your average guy who doesn't mind helping out. To tell you the truth, I wish they would just put me to work on the trains. It would be a lot easier." [Mur00]

- A 29-year-old subway booth clerk was arrested after selling counterfeit Metrocards to investigators. He had apparently discovered a way to create fake but still valid access cards. [TPM01]

- A collection of 17 people, including five workers at Intel and a former Microsoft employee, were arrested for trading pirated copies of software. Many of the copies came from company machines. The former

Microsoft employee "allegedly gave access to Microsoft's internal network to the ringleader." [unk00b]

- Emulex's shares dropped more than $50 in 15 minutes after bad news claiming that the company was restating it's earnings hit the Bloomberg network. It was triggered by a fake press release. [Ber00]

- In 2000, an ex-system administrator for a Navy contractor was found guilty of placing a "time bomb" in the computer system, apparently after being demoted. The assistant U.S. attorney prosecuting the case said, "(Omega) had relied on (him) for security, but, unfortunately, it was the fox watching the chicken coop." Losses were estimated to be $10 million. [unk00a]

- A pair of Brooklyn-based New York City police officers apparently spent their spare time robbing drug dealers and businesses. According to the New York Times, relying upon information provided by "federal authorities", "the pair, using a mobile computer in their police car, tracked down the detective's home address and drove by with an accomplice in tow to plan his murder." [Ras01]

- A Justice Department report found that banks and other information brokers were all too willing to share data. According to the Washington Post, "a review of policies at banks, mutual funds and credit card companies shows that major companies frequently do not require passwords or codes, despite the warnings, because of the expense involved and because officials fear their customers will find the safeguards inconvenient."

- The retired chief of police of Plymouth Township in Michigan told the Detroit Free Press, "I'm not going to be so naive as to say an officer hasn't seen a pretty girl and run her plate." The process is known as "running a plate for a date."[Elr01]

  In one case, the Free Press reported, an officer, "later told the woman he had followed her home the night before, according to police records. He called her by her middle name, which she had not told him. He described her height and weight. And he went on to call her at home and work up to three times a day."

- A DMV employee in Virginia was allegedly caught accepting $10,000 to provide learner's permits to people who didn't sit for the test or provide identification. The investigation began after it was discovered that clerks helped some of the terrorists involved in the September 11 attack. According to the Washington Post, investigators said "He indicated he did not spend any money on himself but gave the money to individuals in need." The clerk denied everything. [Jac01]

Chapter 2

One-Way Functions

Many algorithms in this book depend upon *one-way functions* to scramble the data and provide translucency. These are mathematical functions that are easy to compute but hard to invert. You can compute the answer in one way, but not in reverse.

Many of the basic arithmetic functions are two-way. We know how to multiply two numbers together and reverse the process with division. Addition is balanced by subtraction. Some of the stranger equations, though, are easy to do in one direction but practically impossible to run in reverse.

This chapter explains some of these one-way functions, while later ones describe how to put them into use. The basic trick is straightforward. User scrambles their data with a one-way function before storing it in the database. If someone breaks into the database, the attacker can't find the users' information because the functions run in only one direction. The database is useless to the attacker because one-way functions protect the contents.

Users, however, can always access their data. In most cases, the user holds a password or other relatively secret information. This information is scrambled to produce some key or index to the information in the database. Users can rescramble their data and refind their information because they know their passwords.

The simplest example is the password database of a computer that contains the password scrambled by a one-way function. Every time a user presents a password, it is scrambled and compared to the database. No one can take the database and reverse the one-way function, so the database remains secure. Users, though, can always get access.

For the sake of simplicity, let $h(x)$ stand for a one-way function. This is common because one important class of one-way functions is also called *hash functions* or more properly *cryptographically secure hash functions*. Many computer scientists and database administrators know the term *hash function* as a tool for evenly distributing data throughout a file. The cryptographically secure hash functions in this book accomplish that goal *and* protect information by being computable in only one direction. For the rest of the book, assume that the term *hash function* is shorthand for a hash function that is also one-way or cryptographically secure.

One-way functions come in many different forms:

Pure One-Way Functions These are particular mathematical equations where it is easy to compute $h(x)$, but practically impossible to take a value of y and find a value of x such that $y = h(x)$. These functions often grow exponentially more difficult to reverse as the size of the values increases. This means that f may not be one-way for small values of x and y, but it is relatively easy to find large enough values where it is nearly impossible to invert f.

Unfortunately, none of the one-way functions come with absolute mathematical proof that they can be computed in only one direction. No one has publicly described solutions to the functions in this book. This doesn't mean that they don't exist, but many minds have pursued the answers. Several rich prizes await anyone who would describe how to solve several of the most famous problems.

On the other hand, many one-way functions protect valuable economic information. A life of crime for someone who discovers the answer could also be a temptation.

Trapdoor Functions These are one-way functions to the average person, but two-way to those who know a particular secret called the *trapdoor* or, more properly, a *key*. The functions are usually called *public-key encryption*, a term that describes an encryption function that uses one key to encrypt the data and another to decrypt it. One key is made public, and the other is kept private.

Many database experts use the word "key" to refer to a value used to look up a particular row. This book generally uses it as a value used to unlock encrypted data.

These functions are not properly one-way because anyone who knows the private key can reverse them. Some translucent databases may need to include trapdoors like this. The average user may not be able to reverse the scrambling, but a power user with the right private key will have access.

In general, including trapdoors runs counter to the principle of minimizing access to information. They are included here, though, for the sake of completeness. Sometimes they might provide an ideal compromise.

Secret-Key Encryption Basic encryption functions scramble data using a key. If you know the key, you can get the data. These are sometimes called *symmetric encryption* because of that balance. These functions produce well-scrambled, inscrutable data, but anyone with access to the secret key can unlock it.

These are not one-way functions because they use the same key to scramble and unscramble data. Anyone scrambling data must also have the ability to unscramble it. That is a potentially large weakness if many people must use the database.

Many databases already offer to encrypt either all or parts of the information. This technique is straight-forward and very useful in some situations. It is not as elegant nor as novel as the solutions using pure one-way functions, at least in the opinion of the author.

The secret key functions are included here because they may serve as a compromise in the right situation.

For most intents, the pure one-way functions, the trapdoor functions, and the secret key functions can be interchanged. The algorithms still provide the same level of security, but adding secret trapdoors can offer some people extra access.

In many cases, there's no practical reason to provide extra access by using impure functions. If you're going to build a translucent database, you're already considering losing access to some data. Why not lose it altogether?

Each database designer will come to an individual conclusions about this matter. Some may prefer to use trapdoor functions because they like the extra freedom to sneak a peek, *just in case*. Others want to absolve themselves of all responsibility. Any trapdoor or key can be compromised. The pure functions scramble the data so it can't be reversed, and the operation is final.

Most secret key functions can also be turned into pure one way functions if used in a particular way. See Section 2.3.1.

You say, "It is dark." And in truth, I did place a cloud before your sun. But do you not see how the edges of the cloud are already glowing and turning light.
–Friedrich Nietzsche

2.1 Pure One-Way Functions

There are any number of one-way functions available, but choosing the most common is often a good bet. There is no mathematical proof that any of the functions are truly one-way, so choosing popular, well-studied functions are the best way to ensure that there is no way to reverse them. We are much more likely to know about attacks on popular functions than on less popular ones.

There are really two kinds of pure functions: natural and synthetic. That is really a disingenuous term because all functions are created by their authors. But some seem more like generic mathematics. The first function, the discrete log, looks like something from algebra class. The second function, the SHA, was created ex nihilio to act as a one-way function. For this reason, the first feels a bit more natural and the second seems more synthetic. If instinct is worth anything in mathematics, I feel that synthetic functions are more likely to be secure because they are designed to be purely one-way. But no one should put much stock in instinct because numbers can be especially strange.

2.1.1 Discrete Log

One of the most popular one-way functions is often called the *discrete logarithm* or *discrete log*. If x is an integer less than a prime number p, then

$g^x \bmod p$ is easy to compute. But given a value of y, it is hard to find the value of x that produces $y = g^x \bmod p$. That is, it is hard to find the log of y.

The value of g can be any integer less than p, but some are better than others. The best are known as *generators* because they generate every value less than p. That is, for every $y \leq p$, there is some i such that $y = g^i \bmod p$. If thats holds for all y, then g is a generator.

Here's a quick example that shows all values of g^x where $g = 2$ and $p = 11$:

x	2^x	$2^x \bmod 11$
2	4	4
3	8	8
4	16	5
5	32	10
6	64	9
7	128	7
8	256	3
9	512	6
10	1024	1

There is a good algorithm that computes $g^x \bmod p$ given x, but there is no known fast solution for reversing the operation. That is not apparent when the values are as small as $p = 11$, but the difference becomes notable as p grows larger.

Here is the algorithm for computing $g^x \bmod p$. The main loop is repeated once for every bit in p, and the number of bits in p is equal to the log base two of p.

1. Set $a = 1$, $c = 2$, and $i = 0$.

2. Let $\{b_0, b_1 \ldots b_{k-1}\}$ be a binary representation of x where b_0 is the least significant bit.

3. Repeat this loop k times.

   (a) If b_i is 1, set a to be $ac \bmod p$.

   (b) Square c modulo p.

   (c) Increment i.

4. Return the answer a.

There are several good algorithms for reversing this process, but all of them take time proportional to the size of p, not $\log_2 p$. This means that the discrete log problem is effectively one-way as p grows to have 2048 or more bits. 2^{2048} is a very large number. New mathematical insight may change that, but until it arrives we can presume that this is a one-way function for sufficiently large values.

Many libraries and toolkits include functions for working with extremely long integers that may have thousands of bits. Java, for instance, includes the `BigInteger` class which provides a way to compute $g^x \bmod p$ efficiently. While these implementations are generally much faster than the job of inverting them, they are still slow compared with other one-way functions. The SHA function described in the next section is much faster than computing the $g^x \bmod p$.

The discrete log is used as a one-way function by converting any string or array of bytes into one long integer, x, and then finding a value of p larger than all possible values of x. That can be cumbersome when x varies in size or grows exceptionally large. One solution is to split x into smaller parts. The other is to use a more flexible hash function ,like SHA.

Oh, one last note on terminology. Technically, we use *discrete exponentiation* as the one-way function and rely on the strength of the discrete log problem for security. One is easy, the other hard. Despite the inaccuracy this book will often refer to discrete log one-way functions even though it might be more proper to use the term discrete exponentiation.

2.1.2 The Secure Hash Algorithm (SHA)

The *secure hash algorithm, SHA*, is an algorithm validated by the National Institute of Standards and Technology for acting as a one-way function. The development team based most of it's work on known public contributions like Ron Rivest's MD-5 algorithm but also relied upon some of the highly secretive mathematicians at the National Security Agency. Some argue that the contribution of highly trained cryptographers from the government labs helped create an even better function while some worry that they may have slipped in some hidden weaknesses. While there's no way to prove that there are no weaknesses, all of the evidence suggests that the NSA saw a strong hash function as an important part of the American information infrastructure.

The SHA function takes a file of any length less than 2^{64} bits and produces a 160-bit value in response. SHA is a one-way function, which means that given y, it should be hard to find a value of x so that $y = SHA(x)$. If arbitrarily long files can be fed into SHA, it should not be hard to prove that there are many files that produce the same result. These are known as *hash collisions*. While these collisions are an undesirable weakness, the odds suggest that they don't happen very often. The odds suggest about one matched pair should emerge if you assemble a set of 2^{80} values, a very large number.

The arbitrary size of the SHA input is both a blessing and a curse. On one hand, there's no need to plan ahead. The function will accept long names, short names and almost anything else. Cryptographers often call $SHA(x)$ the *message digest* because it provides a surrogate for the message itself.

The existence of collisions, however rare, continues to worry some users. The fact that two people, two files or two strings could have the same value of *SHA* could cause trouble in some odd cases. Banks, governments and careful people everywhere don't like to play the odds, even when they're as long as one in 2^{80}. In these cases, it makes more sense to use one-way functions like the discrete log.

The SHA function itself looks like a giant numerical blender. Data is processed in 512-bit chunks or, more correctly, 16 blocks of 32 bits. There are 80 rounds in which four different functions, f_1, f_2, f_3, and f_4, scramble the bits in one of the different blocks. The functions are chosen to be both nonlinear and easily computed by a modern CPU. They are:

$$
\begin{aligned}
f_1(x, y, z) &= (x \otimes y) \odot ((\ominus x) \otimes z) \\
f_2(x, y, z) &= x \oplus y \oplus z \\
f_3(x, y, z) &= (x \otimes y) \odot (x \otimes z) \odot (y \otimes z) \\
f_4(x, y, z) &= x \oplus y \oplus z
\end{aligned}
$$

In the equations above, $\otimes$ represents boolean AND, $\oplus$ stands for XOR, $\odot$ represents OR, and $\ominus$ represents NOT. Notice that $f_4 = f_2$ and that there are really three distinct functions, but they are applied in four different passes so the terminology makes some sense.

The details of SHA aren't worth summarizing here. The data is loaded into the registers and scrambled by repeated applications of f_1, f_2, f_3 and f_4. Between each round, the blocks are rotated by seemingly arbitrary amounts to increase the mixing. In the end, the results are so scrambled that it should be impossible to reverse the process.

There is no mathematical proof or guarantee that SHA is a pure one-way function, but the designers did rely upon the results of others who have attacked similar functions, like MD-5. The knowledge of those attacks led to changes that added more strength to SHA.

Computing the SHA is relatively fast, at least several orders of magnitude as fast as computing discrete log. That makes it popular for most uses of one-way functions.

2.1.3   MD-5

The *MD-5* algorithm is a precursor to the Secure Hash Algorithm. It is functionally similar, although some believe that it is a bit less secure. It is a useful choice because no serious flaws have been found after years of common use. Many databases, for instance, offer MD5 functions but haven't implemented SHA yet. For most purposes, the casual user can still treat them as functionally equivalent as long as they are aware that there are some differences.

2.2   Public Key Functions

Much of the first research into one-way functions and trapdoor functions began with the quest for an encryption solution with two keys: one for encrypting and one for decrypting. This interest in *asymmetric encryption* exploded in the mid-1970s after researchers at Stanford and MIT found the first effective solutions.

This book is not interested in public-key encryption per se. There are many applications for the technology itself, and it would be distracting to explore all of them. This book will concentrate on how to use public-key encryption as one-way functions with trapdoors.

One of the most successful trapdoor/public-key encryption functions was developed by Ron Rivest, Adi Shamir and Len Adleman. [RRA78] It is similar to the discrete log problem described in Section 2.1.1 because it also relies upon arithmetic computed modulo some large number. In this case, the large number is the product of two primes, p and q, not a single prime. The strength still comes from the fact that it is easy to raise a number to a power, but it is hard to run that operation in reverse. There is no known way to take the discrete log of a value modulo either a prime or the product of two large primes.

Chapter 10 describes how to use these functions to create digital signatures that can authenticate a database.

RSA uses two keys: one for encryption and one for decryption. Call the first e and the second d. If they are constructed correctly, you can encrypt a message, x, by computing $x^e \bmod n$. This result can be decrypted by raising it to the d power; that is, by computing $(x^e \bmod n)^d \bmod n = x^{ed} \bmod n$. The values of e and d are chosen so that $x^{ed} \bmod n = x$.

Finding a pair of values, e and d, is easy if you know the factorization of $n = pq$. Pick one and then choose the other so that $e \times d = 1 \bmod (p-1)(q-1)$. At this point, there is no other general way to find a pair from n alone without knowing the factorization. There are some specific keys that are weak, but the description of them is beyond the scope of this book. The odds of encountering one are low if the values of p and q are chosen at random. A typical public key consists of the values n and e. The corresponding private key is d.

The RSA function makes a good one-way function with a trapdoor. Anyone can compute $x^e \bmod n$, but only the person holding d can invert this value to find x. Sometimes the value of d can even be discarded just after creation to ensure that this remains a pure one-way function. There's no easy way to determine d from just the values of e and n.

This approach has many of the same advantages and disadvantages as the discrete log function. The value of n must be larger than any value x, or the data must be broken up into smaller parts. Functions like SHA are still faster because exponentiation modulo pq is close to as complex as exponentiation modulo n. (Some operations can be accelerated if you know the individual values of p and q.)

2.3 Secret-Key Functions

Secret-key functions are some of the basic workhorses in cryptography. They take some data x and a key k and scramble the data so that only someone who knows k can unscramble it. Let $f_k(x)$ stand for encryption and $f_k^{-1}(x)$

This book uses "secret" to refer to the key from a symmetrical function like the AES and "private" to refer to the hidden keys in asymmetrical or public-key encryption.

stand for decryption. The functions use one key that must be present for both encryption and decryption.

Some of the most common secret-key functions are the Data Encryption Standard, Rijndael, Blowfish and RC-4, although there are many others. One of the most popular today is Rijndael because it was chosen by the National Institute of Standards and Technology to serve as the Advanced Encryption Standard, or AES. The selection process attracted more than a dozen entries and lasted more than several years. NIST solicited many papers at public conferences before choosing Rijndael from a group of five finalists. If you're looking for a good secret-key function you might also consider the other four finalists: MARS, RC6, Serpent, and Twofish.

There is not enough space to describe the design of these secret key functions. In the most abstract sense, they interleave *confusion* with *diffusion* to provide security. The functions create confusion by scrambling some part of the data with a non-linear function like the ones used in SHA. The functions add diffusion by rearranging the bits in the data to ensure that the value of each part is "confused" with another. The functions themselves are similar to SHA and MD-5 in structure and spirit.

Secret-key functions are used extensively in databases to provide security. Many databases provide a way to encrypt a particular column or table with a set key. These can provide the most basic level of translucency because only the person knowing the key can operate upon the data. This approach is often quite useful, but it has weaknesses. The database must get the key itself to operate. If someone intercepts it, then the data is compromised.

Many algorithms in this book are more secure because the database never uses any of the keys. Pure one-way functions like SHA have no keys, and functions like RSA can scramble data with only one key. After the scrambling is done, the matching and database operations work with scrambled data alone. They don't need the key either.

Speed is one major advantage of secret key functions. The best functions, like Rijndael, are blazing fast compared with functions like RSA. If you need a fast method with a trapdoor, then you might consider secret-key encryption to be a one-way function. The fact that the same key is used for both encryption and decryption is often a serious limit.

2.3.1 Turning a Secret-Key Function Into a Pure One-Way Function.

Secret-key encryption functions can be turned into cryptographically secure hash functions with a simple trick. Each secret-key function uses keys of a certain size. Assume we're using AES, which takes 80 bits in the simplest form. Break the data for the one-way function into 80-bit blocks: $k_1, k_2 \ldots k_n$.

Let c_0 be some arbitrary constant chosen by all users. Let $c_i = f_{k_i}(c_{i-1})$. This produces a chain of values that are encrypted by parts of the data being passed through the one-way function. The last value, c_n, is the result.

This system works as a one-way function because given x and y, it should be difficult to find a value of k that produces the right value from the encryption: $y = f_k(x)$. If you can accomplish that, you can break the secret-key encryption function.

There are few practical reasons to use a secret-key function like Rijndael in this way. Most hash functions, like SHA, are faster and better at acting like a one-way function. The only reason to use a construction like that is when SHA is not available but a good secret-key function is.

2.3.2 Turning One-Way Functions Into Secret-Key Encryption Functions

Let's say you have a one-way function, $h(x)$, but you want to use it as a secret-key function, $f_k(x)$. Let $k_0 = k$ and $k_i = h(k_{i-1})$. This produces a stream of bits that should be fairly random. If the one-way function is any good, it will be impossible to guess k_{i-1} from k_i. The value of x can be encrypted by XOR'ing it with this stream of values $\{k_0, k_1 \ldots\}$. Split x into blocks of the same size as k. Call them $\{x_0, x_1 \ldots\}$. $f_{k_i}(x_i) = x_i \oplus k_i$. The entire result can be concatenated together.

That approach has some weaknesses. Anyone who can unscramble one of the blocks, can recover k_i and then decrypt all of the following blocks. This weakness can be avoided by discarding a number of bits at each step. Assume we're using SHA, a one-way function that produces 160-bit results. Instead of using all 160 bits as k_i, we could only use 80 bits if x is broken up into 80 bit blocks. Anyone who unscrambles one block would still be forced to guess 80 bits to unscramble the following ones.

2.4 Implementations

Many databases incorporate one-way functions into their version of SQL. The extra functions make it simple for a database programmer to create a translucent database without doing any extra programming. Many of the databases themselves use one of the functions to scramble their own passwords controlling access.

2.4.1 MySQL

MySQL includes a few important functions that can provide one-way protection, but the standard manual does not offer much documentation. These functions can be used in SQL queries with the database. The computation is done at the database simplifying the client, but offering more weaknesses for eavesdroppers.

MD5("data") The MD5 function takes an arbitrary string, hashes it using the MD5 algorithm and returns a 32-character-long string representing the

Now an allegory is but a translation of abstract notions into a picture-language, which is itself nothing but an abstraction from objects of the senses; the principal being more worthless even than its phantom proxy, both alike unsubstantial, and the former shapeless to boot. On the other hand, a symbol is characterized by a translucence of the special in the individual, or of the general in the special, or of the universal in the general; above all though the translucense of the eternal through and in the temporal. It always partakes of the reality which it renders intelligible; and while it enunciates the whole, abides itself as a living part in that unity of which it is the representative.
–Samuel Taylor Coleridge *"The Statesman's Manual"*

value in hexadecimal.

The line:

```
INSERT INTO test VALUE(MD5('spot'));
```

adds the value b2e189abf85e809a51522cdb0e53083a to a text field. Notice that the results come as the ASCII character, not a binary representation of the bytes. This is easier to read and use, but it takes up twice as much space.

PASSWORD("password") This is the function used by MySQL to store passwords to control access. It accepts a string and returns a 16-character string containing a hexadecimal representation of the value. MySQL explicitly claims that it uses a different password mechanism than UNIX.

If you want to create a new user, you would issue a command like:

```
INSERT INTO USER VALUES("localhost","fred",PASSWORD("toma-
to"))
```

.

ENCODE("Data goes here","password here") MySQL also includes a generic ENCODE function for encrypting and decrypting data. The result emerges as a binary value so it should be stored as a BLOB.

```
INSERT INTO TEST VALUES(ENCODE("secret value","secret pass-
word")
```

DECODE("Data goes here","password here") Reverses the process. If you passed a string into the function, it should return a string.

ENCRYPT("Data goes here","Password") Some versions of MySQL can use the UNIX crypt function with this. To decrypt, use the same ENCRYPT function with, of course, the right password.

DES_ENCRYPT **and** DES_DECRYPT Version 4.0 of MySQL will come with functions that offer DES scrambling. The implementation includes a feature that mimics one of the more useful features of public-key encryption with this secret key algorithm.

A user can store up to 10 different keys for the database. Another user, perhaps without access to the keys, can ask that data be encrypted by one of these ten keys. The database will perform the operation without revealing the key to user. In the future, only a person with access to the key can recover this value. This allows users with basic access to perform encryption that can only be understood by someone else. This is not the same as public-key, but it can be a practical alternative.

2.4.2 PostgreSQL

PostgreSQL added an MD5 hashing function with version 7.2.

2.4.3 Oracle

Oracle offers a wide range of encryption algorithms created and tested by some of the best minds in the business. They include sophisticated tools integrated into a number of different layers. The company itself is very sensitive to the problems of security and the employees routinely devote a great deal of thought to protecting information from the wrong eyes. The techniques in this book can be combined with the basic Oracle tools to provide even better protection.

Most of these routines are encapsulated in the Oracle Advanced Security toolkit that started appearing in Oracle 7 and continues through Oracle9i. The system provides a number of different tools for protecting the connection to the database and encrypting some of the information in it. Most of the toolkit is designed to encrypt the link between the central database and any clients or satellites that make a connection.

All of these techniques may be useful, but readers of this book will be most interested in the functions encapsulated in the DBMS_OBFUSCATION_TOOLKIT. These are:

DESEncrypt Encrypts data using the U.S. Government's Data Encryption Standard (DES). This takes a 7 byte key (56 bits). The parameters can be provided as either RAW or VARCHAR2.

DESDecrypt Decrypts data using the U.S. Government's Data Encryption Standard (DES).

DES3Encrypt Encrypts data three times using the U.S. Government's Data Encryption Standard (DES). This takes a $3 \times 56 = 168$ bit or 21 byte key to provide additional security. It is widely assumed that regular DES encryption is no longer secure in part because some clever people have built machines that can crack it in a day. [Way92, Fou98]

DES3Decrypt Decrypts data encrypted three times with the U.S. Government's Data Encryption Standard (DES).

MD5 This uses the MD5 algorithm on either RAW or VARCHAR2 data to produce a cryptographically secure checksum.

These functions are invoked in PL/SQL with the toolkit's name as an object like this:

```
dbms_obfuscation_toolkit.md5(data)
```

Several other companies offer toolkits that expand Oracle's capabilities. Application Security Inc. (www.appsecinc.com), for instance, sells one package including 25 major algorithms.

2.4.4   Client-side Applications

Using SQL functions to scramble the data makes life easier for the database programmer. The code is easy to write, edit and maintain. Often, the only thing that needs to be done to add translucency is to insert a new function like MD5.

This simple solution is quite secure. Once the data is inserted into the database, the original information is presumably discarded. It may hang around in memory for some time, but it will surely be overwritten or erased soon enough. There will be no unscrambled information available to anyone who gains access to the database afterwards.

If you are also concerned about eavesdroppers or others who might compromise the central server, the best solution is to scramble the data at the client. Libraries including encryption and hashing functions are easy to link into any application.

This approach can also lower the workload of the central database server by letting each client computer handle the encryption and the hashing.

Java applets are particularly useful tools for these remote operations. They can solicit information, check it for correctness, scramble it and then insert it into the database.

This example shows a simple Java applet that fetches a password and scrambles it using an MD5 class created by Santeri Paavolainen. The code is distributed under the GNU Library General Public License and readily available in several source trees. The code in these examples use three main methods:

Update This method "hashes" the data. It usually takes a String, but it can also accept arrays of bytes.

clear Resets the internal state. Used at the beginning of each different computation of $h(x)$.

asHex Returns the result as a hexadecimal String. Useful for storing as a Text element in a database.

When the button pushMe is pressed, method pushMeActionPerformed is invoked to grab the text of the password and hash it. The simplest way a query produced in pushMeActionPerformed can be delivered to a remote database is by inserting it into an HTTP request, a topic that is left out of this example for clarity.

```java
/*  TestTranslucencyApplet.java */
import java.awt.*;
import java.awt.event.*;
import java.applet.*;
public class TestTranslucencyApplet extends Applet
{
  java.awt.Label label1 = new Label();
  java.awt.TextField passwordField = new TextField();
  java.awt.Button pushMe = new Button();
  MD5 hashWithMe=new MD5();
  boolean isStandalone = false;
// Initialize the applet
public void init() {
  try {
    initComponents();
  } catch (Exception e) {
   e.printStackTrace();
  }
}
public void initComponents() throws Exception {
  label1.setText("Password:");
  label1.setLocation(new java.awt.Point(10, 10));
  label1.setAlignment(Label.RIGHT);
  label1.setVisible(true);
  label1.setSize(new java.awt.Dimension(70, 20));
  passwordField.setText("swordfish");
  passwordField.setLocation(new java.awt.Point(90, 10));
  passwordField.setVisible(true);
  passwordField.setSize(new java.awt.Dimension(104, 23));
  pushMe.setLocation(new java.awt.Point(20, 40));
  pushMe.setLabel("Open Sesame");
  pushMe.setVisible(true);
  pushMe.setSize(new java.awt.Dimension(130, 20));
  setLocation(new java.awt.Point(0, 0));
  setLayout(null);
  setSize(new java.awt.Dimension(245, 106));
  add(label1);
  add(passwordField); add(pushMe);
  pushMe.addActionListener(new ActionListener() {
  public void actionPerformed(ActionEvent e) {
    pushMeActionPerformed(e);
  } });
}
public void pushMeActionPerformed(ActionEvent e) {
   hashWithMe.clear(); // restart the MD5
  hashWithMe.Update(passwordField.getText());
  // hash the password
  String query="INSERT INTO table VALUES";
  query=query+"(\""+hashWithMe.asHex()+"\");";
  // do something with the query.
  }
}
```

2.5 Conclusions

One-way functions are tools that scramble data, x, so that it is practically impossible to reverse it. That is, there's no easy way to take a value of y and find x so that $y = h(x)$. These functions are quite useful for databases because they can obscure data without preventing searching and matching.

Pure one-way functions have no known trapdoors or loopholes. One-way functions built out of public-key or secret-key encryption functions can provide these trapdoors if called for.

2.5.1 Lessons

- One-way functions are easy to compute, but practically impossible to invert or undo.

- When people say "practically impossible", they often mean using numbers that are a bit larger and longer than normal.

- The ideal one-way functions provide a unique answer for each input. $h(x) = 0$ is easy to compute, impossible to invert, but practically useless.

- Many practical one-way functions are close to providing a unique answer. The Secure Hash Algorithm, SHA, takes all input and returns a 160-bit number. There are 2^{160} possible answers. Many inputs produce the same output, but it is practically impossible to find any x and y where $h(x) = h(y)$ and $x \neq y$.

- In most cases, "practically impossible" means that no one has publicly described how to compute some function in a reasonable amount of time. There may be someone with secret knowledge.

- One-way functions provide surrogates for the data. Instead of placing the sensitive value x in the database, put $h(x)$. You can still search for x by searching for $h(x)$, but a casual browser won't be able to find x from $h(x)$.

- One-way functions also provide summaries. Large files can be fed into a cryptographically secure hash function like SHA and only 160 bits come out. The slightest change in the file will dramatically change the character of the answer. For this reason, some people use the functions to produce values they call *message digests* or *message authentication codes*.

- Exponentiation modulo a prime number is a popular one-way function. It is easy to compute $g^x \bmod p$, but practically impossible to reverse by taking what is known as the *discrete log*.

- Some one-way functions have backdoors. These are often called *public-key encryption*. Anyone can use a public value, known as the public key, but only someone who knows the private key can invert the function.

Chapter 3

One-Way Tables

The one-way functions from Chapter 2 are easy to put to work scrambling data. The basic solutions are simple to use, but paying attention to a few details can help anticipate and eliminate some potentially annoying problems produced by the one-way functions. Making a database translucent can be as easy as inserting the function call MD5 into your SQL query, but doing a good job calls for paying attention to potential headaches.

The biggest problem with translucent databases is the fact that their greatest strength, their security, is also a big impediment to debugging. Dealing with slight inconsistencies, mistakes or errors can be close to impossible because the one-way functions scramble the data so effectively. A good hash function, h, should ensure that the values of $h(\textit{"Robert"})$, $h(\textit{"Bob"})$, $h(\textit{"BOB"})$ and $h(\textit{"bob"})$ are wildly different. That prevents attackers from gaining any information from examining the database, but it also blocks debugging.

Translucent databases are not fragile, but they can be annoying and frustrating for users who don't follow directions exactly. People don't always type exactly the same thing. While most people can understand that computers treat "Robert" and "Bob" as different strings, it can be difficult to keep straight the various forms of capitalization ("Bob" versus "bob"). Spaces, punctuation and abbreviation cause even more trouble. ("St. George", "St George", and "Saint George" are very different after being passed through a one-way function.)

Building a good translucent database means anticipating and solving these potential problems. Many of the solutions are quite good. Although they may not be perfect, they can eliminate many of the basic typographical problems confounding users.

Good implementations do more than anticipate potential errors. Translucent databases using one-way functions can also be weaker than they may seem if they aren't designed correctly. A few simple changes to the way that a one-way function is used can add a great deal of security to the database itself. The one-way function may be completely secure, but missteps in passing data to it can introduce weaknesses.

Sometimes, these two problems are at odds with each other. Adding more flexibility to the database can reduce the security. Removing the flexibility can make attacks more difficult. The trick is to add enough flexibility without reducing security below a reasonable level.

3.1   An Example from a Department Store

Adding translucency to a database is as simple as passing some values through a one-way function before storing them in the database. Imagine you run the data center for a large clothing store. To improve customer service you would like to provide a way for customers to look up their past purchases. A customer may like a particular pair of shoes or pants enough to buy another pair. To encourage this repeat business, you decide to create a database that stores the customer's purchases and the sizes chosen. If the shoes in Size 10 fit like a glove, then the same size can be ordered again. The customer doesn't need to remember which size of which style fits well.

This is a perfect opportunity to add translucency. Clothing sizes are not serious, classified military information, but some people are sensitive about the dimensions of their waists. They might prefer not have that information readily available on the Internet.

The information is also not crucial to the store's business. There is no solid reason why a store needs to know who bought what when. Once a customer goes out the door, information about the choices they made is only of interest to that person. The store can do quite well with a basic statistical analysis noting how many units were sold of each size and style.

Building a translucent database balances these needs. The customer gets access to information about past purchases without military-grade security system to protect modesty. The store provides a service without taking on a heavy responsibility.

Here's a sample SQL command to create a table:

```
CREATE TABLE purchases (nameHash CHAR(32), prNum INTEGER,
size1 VARCHAR(8), size2 VARCHAR(8), size3 VARCHAR(8),
orderMade DATETIME, orderShipped DATETIME);
```

The table holds the product information (prNum); the length, width, height, inseam or whatever (size1, size2 and size3) and the dates the orders were made and fulfilled (orderMade and orderShipped). The name is stored in the column nameHash, a 32-character string created by applying MD5 to the person's name.

Here are a few lines that insert records after Fred Smith and Bob Jones buy a pair of pants and some shoes:

```
INSERT INTO purchases VALUES(MD5("Fred Smith"), 55424, "32",
"34", "", NOW(), NULL);
```

```
INSERT INTO purchases VALUES(MD5("Bob Jones"), 55424, "36",
"32", "", NOW(), NULL);

INSERT INTO purchases VALUES(MD5("Fred Smith"), 33212,
"10.5", "", "", NOW(), NULL);

INSERT INTO purchases VALUES(MD5("Bob Jones"), 33212,
"12.0", "", "", NOW(), NULL);
```

Here's what the database table looks like:

nameHash	prodNum	size1	size2	orderMade
e087aa7eade9b41ebd0063e64ec5c89c	55424	32	34	2001-11-16 10:46:33
60d38aa9b65aa940b10b6a9dceaea1b9	55424	36	32	2001-11-16 10:48:23
e087aa7eade9b41ebd0063e64ec5c89c	33212	10.5		2001-11-16 10:49:21
60d38aa9b65aa940b10b6a9dceaea1b9	33212	12.0		2001-11-16 10:49:43

Notice that the first and third entries have the same value? They are both entries for Fred Smith's purchases. If Fred returns, he can pull up the records for all his past purchases if they can help him choose the right size.

The security provided by this simple example is good but far from perfect. The information contained in the database is minimal. There is no personal information. If the clerks want to waste a Friday afternoon searching for the name of the customer with the biggest gain in waist size, they'll be disappointed. It is possible to find the customer's hashed name, but not the name itself.

The database is still useful to the purchasers planning which sizes to order next year. The product numbers and sizes are kept in the clear. It is also possible for the marketing department to discover that products 55424 and 33212 are very popular combinations.

But there are also weaknesses. If you want to look up Fred Smith's information, you just need to type in his name:

```
SELECT * FROM purchases WHERE nameHash=MD5("Fred Smith");
```

The information comes pouring out if you know the right name, capitalization and punctuation. That may be an appropriate level of protection for data like this. People can quickly look up their files, but clerks and others can't troll for names.

3.1.1 Adding Security

The simplest mechanism for adding security is to add a password or a key. The user can choose a password and have the result hashed with the name:

```
INSERT INTO purchases VALUES(MD5("Fred Smith/swordfish") ,
55424, "32", "34","",NOW(),NULL);
```

That scheme makes it is impossible to look up Fred Smith's record without knowing the password, "swordfish". If it's not added, the one-way function's results won't be correct. Mr. Smith must now remember a password to use the result. Incidentally, the slash ("/") is not necessary. It's just included to make reading the code a bit easier. Any punctuation scheme can be used as long as it is consistent.

Passwords are not the only way to reduce access. Another solution is to add more personal information to the hash like the person'saddress, Social Security number and favorite football team or other information. The only limit is the patience and forbearance of the customers.

```
INSERT INTO purchases VALUES(MD5("Fred Smith/1313
Mockingbird Lane/014-33-4421/Scorpio/Pittsburg Steelers")
,55424, "32", "34", "", NOW(),NULL);
```

The result is a long mixture that may not be as hard to remember as a password but is very difficult for a snoop to get correct.

3.2 Cleaning Up One-Way Input

one-way functions, cleaning up input lower case alphabets, ambiguity in one-way input upper case alphabets, ambiguity in one-way input

Many strings say the same thing while looking wildly different to the computer. "Robert", "Bob" and "bob" are simple examples. Users often discover even better ambiguities to try the souls of programmers. Street names like "St. George's St." confuse computers trying to determine what the "St." abbreviates.

Simple software can ignore these problems and leave it up to the user to type in exactly the same thing every time. That is not the best solution, but it takes little time to build. It also trains the user to type things in exactly the same way each time they are used. That training may be painful, but it exposes the inner pickiness of computers in a way that can be useful to humans capable of adapting. The solution may not be ideal, but at least it is uncomplicated and direct.

Sometimes standard software packages can help create canonical forms. Section 10.2 uses the Java Date classes to put dates and times into a standard format.

Better software can minimize the problems by establishing some canonical order for strings collected from humans by applying a set of transformations that reduce inconsistencies. Here are some useful ones:

- Convert every letter to uppercase. Or convert them all to lowercase. It's your choice. The Java String class includes the methods toUpperCase and toLowerCase, which take optional arguments for tuning the behavior to local languages.

  The SQL functions UCASE and UPPER convert a string to uppercase ASCII, while the functions LCASE and LOWER convert a string to lowercase ASCII.

- Remove leading and trailing spaces. People often include them without realizing that they're there. The Java String class includes the trim function to remove leading and trailing spaces. These SQL functions are more specific:

- LTRIM removes leading spaces.
- RTRIM removes trailing spaces.
- TRIM [BOTH | LEADING | TRAILING] can remove leading characters, trailing characters or both. (TRIM BOTH 'A' FROM 'ALABANZA' returns LABANZ.) If no character is specified, the function assumes a space.

- Remove double spaces from inside the string. Sometimes people insert two space characters by mistake. Adding a double space after a period was once standard practice for typists. Removing double spaces in Java requires writing your own function.

  The SQL command REPLACE(Source String, 'replace me', 'with me') can be repeated several times to replace double spaces with single spaces.

- Remove all spaces and nonprinting characters. Spaces may be important to humans, but they don't matter once the string is passed through a pure one-way function. Stripping out all nonprinting characters eliminates the possibility that someone may skip a space or insert a double space. Sometimes other nonprinting characters, like the carriage return or the new line, can appear. These can be especially troublesome because different operating systems use different combinations of carriage returns and line feeds as the default. If people type the same multiple line string on a UNIX box, a PC and a Macintosh, they will produce slightly different strings.

  Excluding all nonprinting characters is a good practical approach, but it can introduce errors. The strings "carpenter" and "carp enter" are exactly the same.

- Exclude all punctuation marks. Do they matter? In most cases, they don't, but the strings "Pool closed. No swimming." and "Pool closed? No. Swimming!" have very different meanings.

- Convert punctuation marks or special characters to one simple replacement. Stripping out characters can cause more trouble than simply replacing them with an all-purpose replacement like an asterix. The approach can be useful with addresses because people often use punctuation differently. Some use commas where some use periods. Using asterisks to replace them reduces ambiguity without destroying all detail.

- Write a special function to expand potential abbreviations like "St.", "Rd.", "Blvd." with "Street", "Road", and "Boulevard". Or you may choose to enforce a standard set of abbreviations by replacing all occurences of "Street" with "St." Generating that table is often a large challenge and an exercise in exploring the limits of human language.

- Use the Soundex algorithm. The SOUNDEX function in MySQL will convert words into a string that captures the sound of the word in a way that is independent of spelling. The words "wayner" and "wehner" both produce the string "W560" while the strings "raynor" and "rain or" both produce "R560".

Of course, not every application will need to use every reduction rule.

3.2.1   Some Java Code

Here's an example that computes an ID hash code from the name and password entries:

```
public String computeUserID(){
  md.clear();
  String s=nameTextField.getText();
  s=s+passwordTextField.getText();
  StringBuffer sb=new StringBuffer();
  int sLen=s.length();
  char c;
  for (int i=0;i<sLen;i++){
    c=s.charAt(i);
    if (((c>='A') && (c<='Z')) || ((c>='a') && (c<='z'))) {
      sb.append(c);
      }
    }
  md.Update(sb.toString());
  return md.asHex();   }
```

3.3   Security Trade-Offs

Removing spaces, deleting strange characters and eliminating any ambiguity makes life simpler for users *and* for any attacker. If a particular translucent database converts all passwords to uppercase before storing them away, then an attacker does not need to try lowercase letters to guess this password. The attacker needs to try only the uppercase strings with no spaces and strange characters. Converting a string to uppercase cuts the amount of work for an attacker in half for every character. There are 26^i possible strings with i uppercase letters in them and 52^i possible strings with i upper or lowercase letters. Passing through digits adds another factor of 10^i, and punctuation creates even more potential complexity. Simplicity, on the other hand, adds insecurity.

Is this a trade-off worth making? If the password, name or other information passed into the hash function is small, the answer is no. Computers are already fast enough to search through all uppercase combinations of 8 to 10 letters in no time at all. When strings grow to 20 or more characters, then the loss is easier to take. 26^{20} is much smaller than 52^{20}, but it is still a formidable number.

Judging the strength or weakness of a particular database can be complicated. Many computer operating systems now include software to encourage or even force users to choose good passwords with characters chosen from a large set, including punctuation, numbers and both uppercase and lowercase letters. A user can be forced to pick a long passphrase filled with odd characters.

But people can't pick their names, the names of the streets on which they live, the names of their states, and many other things. If these values are poured into a one-way function, the results may be easier to guess. Imagine that one field of the database contains the MD5 hash of a person's first name. Most Anglo and European names come from a short list that can be tested quickly. There may be a set of 10,000 names that would cover most people. It may not be mathematically possible to reverse the one-way function itself, but it would be possible to run 10,000 names through the function and then compare them to the entry in question. The one-way function may not be scrutable, but the data may fit an easy pattern susceptible to a brute-force search.

The good news is that estimating the cost of a brute-force search is straight-forward. Computing a one-way function takes a set amount of time, and determining the number of times the one-way function must be repeated is easy to do. The more difficult problem is estimating the strength of your enemy. A desktop machine can easily compute close to a million iterations of a one-way function per second. But customized hardware can do even more. Brute-force searches are easily run in parallel, so twice as many processors finishes twice as fast. How much money and time does an attacker have?

Here's a table of some computed values to help estimate the time it would take to do a brute-force search. The table assumes that a basic processor can compute one million copies of a one-way function in a second, something that is not a very solid estimate. Many functions are slower, and many depend upon the size of the input. There are $60 \times 60 \times 24 = 86,400$ seconds in a day.

Potential Chars. S	# Chars. in entry i	Count S^i	CPU Days to search $S^i/86400$
26	8	2.08×10^{11}	2.41
52	8	5.35×10^{13}	618.75
26	10	1.41×10^{14}	1634
52	10	1.45×10^{17}	1.67×10^6
26	12	9.54×10^{16}	1.10×10^6
52	12	3.91×10^{20}	4.53×10^9

3.3.1 Slowing the One-Way Functions

one-way functions, slowing to add security security trade-offs, slowing one-way functions

The simplest way to add security is to slow the one-way functions used in a database. That solution runs counter to the instinct of many one-way function designers who try to create mathematical contraptions that are both fast and impossible to invert. Using an off-the-shelf function and taking advantage of their hard work and research means settling for a function that is, alas, very efficient.

The easiest way to slow the process is to repeat it any number of times. Instead of storing $h(data)$ in the table, store $h(h(h(h(h(data)))))$. Why stop there? Why not repeat the process 500 or 10,000 times?

The desirability of this solution depends a great deal on the architecture of the system. If you can rely on the clients to compute all of the one-way functions, then hashing the data thousands of times is usually possible. The added load is not noticed. If you rely on the central database server to compute the one-way functions, then arbitrary complexity can bog down the machine. Computing a function twice can double the time to process each query.

3.3.2 Salt

The designers of the UNIX password scrambling mechanism added security by deliberately repeating the scrambling step *and* adding a bit of *salt* to the process. They used that term to refer to a short random string added to each person's password to add great inconvenience to a brute-force attacker.

Imagine that one column of the database is a person's name. For the sake of example, assume that this name is eight uppercase characters. Generating all possible eight uppercase characters should take $26^8 = 2.08 \times 10^{11}$ operations. To make matters worse, two people with the same name will have the same entry in the table. It might be possible to find family members just by sorting the list.

The search process can be thwarted by adding a separate column to the table containing a random number called the salt. This random value is stored in the clear and it is mixed into the result. Instead of storing $h(name)$, the column now stores $h(salt, name)$. If each entry in the database uses a salt value chosen at random, then even entries from people with the same name will be different.

This extra salt slows one common brute-force attack on a database. Computing the one-way hash of all possible eight character names and then searching for their value in the table is now a worthless endeavor. The salt means that each element must be attacked in turn. If there are 10,000 entries in the database, then an attack now takes 2.08×10^{15}.

Not all applications can add salt to the mix. If the processing is done at the client, then the client must know the salt to mix with the name. The first time a name is added to the database, the client can simply create the salt at random. The second time, the client must somehow find the same salt from the database. In the case of a password database, the salt can be recovered by using the user's name, which is stored in the clear.

Salt can't be used if the main way to search a database is also the part scrambled by the one-way function. In Section 3.1, the name is used to recover the records of purchases. Adding salt to the one-way function, $h(salt, name)$, would break the system. There wout be no easy way for the customer to recover the salt upon return. There must be some clear data that can pull the correct record from the database and recover the salt. This isn't always available in many translucent databases designed to protect identities.

3.4   Adding Redundancy

The example in Section 3.1 offers plenty of security against casual browsers, but one error or misspelling can lock a person out of the database. Squeezing out strange characters and converting all the characters to either uppercase or lowercase can avoid many typographical errors, but they can't solve the problems of misspellings or errors.

The database can be made more forgiving by adding extra fields that can help extract data when a few errors are made. Here's an example from a company's human resources department:

```
CREATE TABLE salaries (idHash CHAR(32), salary INTEGER,
sickDays INTEGER, vacationDays INTEGER);
```

The human resources department designs the column idHash to hold $h(name/address/birthdate/SS\#)$ to be extremely careful. A user can look up personal information only by knowing all four fields of information:

```
INSERT INTO salaries VALUES (MD5("Fred Smith/1313
Mockingbird Lane/06-01-1960/012-34-5678"), 60000, 5, 20);
```

This idHash is quite secure, but also subject to a single typing mistake. Abbreviating "Lane" with "Ln", using the wrong birthday or typing in the wrong Social Security number will produce the wrong answer. These lines return nothing:

```
SELECT * FROM salaries WHERE idHash=MD5("Fred Smith/1313
Mockingbird Ln/06-01-1960/012-34-5678");

SELECT * FROM salaries WHERE idHash=MD5("Fred Smith/1313
Mockingbird Ln/06-01-1961/012-34-5678");

SELECT * FROM salaries WHERE idHash=MD5("Fredrick Smith/1313
Mockingbird Ln/06-01-1960/012-34-5678");

SELECT * FROM salaries WHERE idHash=MD5("Fredrick Smith/1313
Mockingbird Ln/06-01-1960/012-34-5679");
```

If Human Resources wants to forgive one error, it can create multiple idHash columns based on subsets of the information. Any match will do. Instead of just using $h(name/address/birthday/SS\#)$, the database might also include other columns with the values $h(name/address/birthday)$, $h(name/birthday/SS\#)$, $h(name/address/SS\#)$, or even $h(address/birthday/SS\#)$:

```
CREATE TABLE salaries2 (hash_nm_ad_bd_ss CHAR(32),
hash_nm_bd_ss CHAR(32), hash_nm_ad_ss CHAR(32), hash_nm_ad_bd
CHAR(32),hash_ad_bd_ss CHAR(32),salary INTEGER, sickDays
INTEGER, vacationDays INTEGER);
```

Information is inserted by creating multiple ID values:

```
INSERT INTO salaries2 VALUES( MD5("Fred Smith/1313
Mockingbird Lane/06-01-1960/012-34-5678"), MD5("Fred
Smith/06-01-1960/012-34-5678"), MD5("Fred Smith/1313
Mockingbird Lane/012-34-5678"), MD5("Fred Smith/1313
Mockingbird Lane/06-01-1960"), MD5("1313 Mockingbird
Lane/06-01-1960/012-34-5678"), 60000,5,20);
```

The result looks like this:

Column	Value
hash_nm_ad_bd_ss	bce75d84a4c522c7387215e067b02ae4
hash_nm_bd_ss	90ea8de5d1e31a68bfdc7ce3a191828b
hash_nm_ad_ss	eacbc6f78f97d87955d9907609865fe0
hash_nm_ad_bd	02a55734e7992d2d9c81f4aebcbf9af4
hash_ad_bd_ss	8ca1d90da9879705bcbb900b5d43f371
salary	60000
sickDays	5
vacationDays	20

This example includes all four possible ID tags that can be created by choosing three of the four fields. You can choose any combination of terms that you want. It might not make sense, for instance, to include hash_ad_bd_ss because it would allow someone to recover the information without knowing the person's correct name. Leaving out hash_nm_ad_bd forces the user to know the Social Security number. Adding the term hash_nm_ss with just two terms would guarantee that the name and the Social Security number be enough.

This query still finds the right value when the address is mistyped:

```
SELECT salary,sickDays,vacationDays FROM salaries2 WHERE
hash_nm_ad_bd_ss= MD5("Fred Smith/1414 Mockingbird
Lane/06-01-1960/012-34-5678") OR hash_nm_bd_ss= MD5("Fred
Smith/06-01-1960/012-34-5678") OR hash_nm_ad_ss= MD5("Fred
Smith/1414 Mockingbird Lane/012-34-5678") OR hash_nm_ad_bd=
MD5("Fred Smith/1414 Mockingbird Lane/06-01-1960");
```

Notice that the column names (hash_nm_ad_bd_ss) use an underscore character (_) to join the names of the fields in a regular way. Using a machine-parsable system like that makes implementing the process simpler. Automating the error-correction process is also possible. That type of introspection makes it possible for generalized software to access translucent databases and infer just which data is processed by which one-way functions.

3.5 An Example with Encryption for Security

The example in Section 3.1 uses the one-way function on one column and leaves the rest of the information in the clear. The department store can use that data without tying it to regular customers. Sometimes the extra information is not really valuable to the store itself. The database is kept around only to help customers.

If the information is not of any value to the store, the data in the other columns can be scrambled, too. One column identifies the data, and the others hold it.

Many databases include the ability to encrypt data as it is inserted and decrypt it as it is retrieved. These functions are useful for many basic applications, but they may not be ideal. The data will travel to and fro in unencrypted form, where they may be snagged by eavesdroppers. The best solution is to encrypt this data at the client's computer to better preserve the principles of translucency.

In this example, the table purchases2 stores the same information as table purchases from Section 3.1. The information is encrypted using MySQL's basic ENCODE and DECODE functions. The data itself is stored in MySQL's TINYBLOB columns, which hold 0 to 255 bytes of data. The variable size is the easiest choice to make because the encryption function operates on round blocks of data. The results are not always the same size as the input.

Here's the SQL statement creating the database:

```
CREATE TABLE purchases2 (nameHash CHAR(32), prNum TINYBLOB,
size1 TINYBLOB, size2 TINYBLOB, size3 TINYBLOB, orderMade
DATETIME, orderShipped DATETIME);
```

Here are four lines inserting the same data again. The password "prodpass" is used to scramble the data:

```
INSERT INTO purchases2 VALUES(MD5("Fred Smith"),
encode("55424", "prodpass"), encode("32", "prodpass"),
encode("34", "prodpass"), "",NOW(), NULL);

INSERT INTO purchases2 VALUES(MD5("Bob Jones"),
encode("55424", "prodpass"), encode("36", "prodpass"),
encode("32", "prodpass"), "",NOW(), NULL);
```

```
INSERT INTO purchases2 VALUES(MD5("Fred Smith"),
encode("33212", "prodpass"), encode("10.5", "prodpass"), "",
"",NOW(),NULL);

INSERT INTO purchases2 VALUES(MD5("Bob Jones"),
encode("33212", "prodpass"), encode("12.0", "prodpass"), "",
"",NOW(),NULL);
```

The data includes plenty of unprintable characters because it is stored as 8-bit quantities that can't be easily converted to ASCII.

```
select nameHash,prNum,size1,orderMade from purchases2;
```

produces:

nameHash	prNum	size1	orderMade
e087aa7eade9b41ebd0063e64ec5c89c	èâòL	Á	2001-11-19 09:01:09
60d38aa9b65aa940b10b6a9dceaea1b9	èâòL	Á	2001-11-19 09:03:31
e087aa7eade9b41ebd0063e64ec5c89c	Á]ÀÖ	$\hat{a} < \hat{o}$	2001-11-19 09:03:36
60d38aa9b65aa940b10b6a9dceaea1b9	Á]ÀÖ	$\hat{a} > n$	2001-11-19 09:03:42

The data can be recovered using the built-in DECODE function.

```
SELECT DECODE(prNum,"prodpass"),DECODE(size1,"prodpass")
FROM purchases2 WHERE nameHash=MD5("Fred Smith");
```

produces:

DECODE(prNum,"prodpass")	DECODE(size1,"prodpass")
55424	32
33212	10.5

There is plenty of flexibility available to whoever will choose the password to scramble the different columns. Using one password to scramble all of them is one of the weakest solutions, although one that is easy to use and remember. Scrambling all entries with the same password makes it possible to extract some limited information from the tables. It's clear, for instance, that only two different product numbers were ordered in this example. This feature might not seem too valuable to an inventory manager, but it might be useful in some context.

Using a different password for each person may make more sense. If the data is valuable enough, the person may want to choose and remember the password. If not, it can be derived from the other information. A simple but very insecure solution is to use the $h(name)$ (nameHash in this example) as the password. The person doesn't need to remember a password, but any attacker can find the password on the same line.

A better solution is to create another password by using a slightly different one-way function on the same information. Instead of using $h(name)$ or $h(name/address/football\ team)$, use $h(P/name)$ where P is some randomly chosen word that ensures that the one-way hash will be different. Computing that takes only one extra step, but it makes it impossible to use $h(name)$

to figure out the password for scrambling the data. The user, however, needs to remember only the same information.

Using a randomly choosen string like P to begin the computation of $h()$ adds some randomness that defends against attackers. This value is hard-coded into the software computing h so the user doesn't need to know it. An attacker who tries to imitate the process can only discover the value of P by examining the software. When the attacker can't see the software itself, this can prevent the attacker from computing $h(P something)$ for any value of *something*. Many of the implementations in this book use this technique. The code in the next section, for instance, uses the phrase "SanDimasHSFootball-Rules". You may want to choose your own.

3.5.1   Some Java Code

Here's another version of the code from Section 3.2.1. This version also allows names and passwords with numbers, mainly for illustration. Notice that the user password is computed with an extra string added to the front: "SanDimasHSFootballRules". That extra string guarantees that the results from `computeUserPassword` will be different from `computeUserID`. The user still fills out the same fields, but the information returned from `computeUserID` will not help us with the password.

```java
public String computeUserPassword(){
  md.clear();
  String s=nameTextField.getText().toUpperCase();
  StringBuffer sb=new StringBuffer();
  int sLen=s.length();
  char c;

  for (int i=0;i<sLen;i++){
    c=s.charAt(i);
    if (((c>='A') && (c<='Z')) || ((c>='0') && (c<='9'))) {
      sb.append(c);
    }
  }

  s=passwordTextField.getText().toUpperCase();
  sLen=s.length();

  for (int i=0;i<sLen;i++){
    c=s.charAt(i);
    if (((c>='A') && (c<='Z')) || ((c>='0') && (c<='9'))){
      sb.append(c);
    }
  }

  md.Update("SanDimasHSFootballRules"+sb);
  return md.asHex();
}
```

3.6   Hashing Instead of Encryption

The example in Section 3.5 encrypted the elements in each column with a password. This makes sense if you want to retrieve the values — something that is often important but not always needed. Sometimes the information is stored in a log file so it can be used for analysis that can be completed with the result of the one-way function.

This example uses a table where multiple columns are passed through a one-way function just to obscure them:

```
CREATE TABLE logfile (tm DATETIME, ipAddress CHAR(32), url
CHAR(32));
```

The time, IP address and URL are stored in the database with statements like this:

```
INSERT INTO logfile VALUES (NOW(), MD5("10.0.1.2"),
MD5("http://www.flyzone.com/"));

INSERT INTO logfile VALUES (NOW(), MD5("10.0.1.2"),
MD5("http://www.flyzone.com/bball/"));

INSERT INTO logfile VALUES
(NOW(),MD5("10.0.1.2"),MD5("http://www.flyzone.com/base/"));
```

This database doesn't store the IP addresses of the visitors nor does it record the URLs they view, but it can still help a Web site administrator keep track of usage. You can still see how many visits come from each IP address each day and you can see how many different URLs that person visits. Unique visitors and unique page views are important counts for advertisers on the Internet. You cannot keep track of individual users and what they read.

That solution is an ideal one for a company gathering Internet ratings. Many people hesitate to take part in surveys that ask for their personal opinions because they wonder how the information may be used. A translucent database like this obscures personal information while still producing useful counts for advertisers.

Simply computing the one-way function of the IP address has weaknesses. If you want to see whether an arbitrary IP address, say, 10.0.1.240, visited the site, then you can compute MD5("10.0.1.240") and look up the information. All visits by that person can be retrieved from the database. The data is still private because the URL is also scrambled, but some information is being leaked.

Plugging that hole is not easy. If you want the table logfile to produce accurate counts of unique visitors and page views, you must ensure that every visit from an IP address will be recorded in the same way. That means you must be consistent in choosing the one-way function.

One possible solution is to use a secret passphrase as part of the insertion processz:

```
INSERT INTO logfile VALUES
(NOW(),MD5("BaltimoreRocks/10.0.1.2"), MD5(
"http://www.flyzone.com/base/"));
```

Adding the phrase "BaltimoreRocks" before the IP address ensures that only someone who knows this passphrase can look up information in the database. You can't simply compute MD5("10.0.1.240") to see whether someone from 10.0.1.240 visited a site, you must compute MD5("BaltimoreRocks/10.0.1.240"). This phrase can't be too secret. Any function adding information to the database must include the phrase, and all of them must use the same one. This is easier to accomplish if the one-way function is computed at the client before it is inserted into the database, not using the built-in functions. An arbitrary hacker or clerk who drills down into the database, though, will not know the password and not be able to recover the information. This secrecy may not be much, but it is often a good habit. It costs little but adds another layer of protection.

3.7   Serial Queries

Replacing a column with the result of a one-way function applied to that information is a good way to add security without destroying all functionality. The average person may not be able to understand that jumble of characters, but the rightful owner can type in the right information and pull up the record. The one problem is that each record looks exactly alike. In Section 3.1, all of Fred Smith's records are stored under the value e087aa7eade9b41ebd0063e64ec5c89c. You might not know that e087aa7eade9b41ebd0063e64ec5c89c is the result of applying the MD5 function to "Fred Smith", but you can see that the same person ordered two items.

Sometimes such patterns are unacceptable. The store may want to know which items were bought by the same consumer, but others may not need that information. A store may want to protect the security of some regular customers by avoiding records showing that the same person comes in every Thursday between 5:00 and 5:20. If you know two or three times that someone ordered items, you could look for patterns in the database in Section 3.1. The order time is stored in the clear, and there may be a good chance that only one customer submitted an order at that time. From that information, you can find the scrambled name (e087aa7eade9b41ebd0063e64ec5c89c) and discover a list of all of the customer's other purchases.

Breaking the link between entries is not hard, but it slows the retrieval process. If a different identification string is used for each row, then an index can't be used to find all transactions quickly. Furthermore, all entries can't be recovered with a query like:

```
SELECT * FROM purchases WHERE
nameHash='e087aa7eade9b41ebd0063e64ec5c89c';
```

Each row must be recovered independently.

Generating a different `nameHash` for each entry is not difficult. Instead of computing $h(name)$ or $h(name/password)$, compute $h(num/name/password)$ where *num* is a value that begins with 1 and increases with each entry.

Let the same SQL command create a new table:

```
CREATE TABLE purchases3 (nameHash CHAR(32), prNum INTEGER,
size1 VARCHAR(8), size2 VARCHAR(8), size3 VARCHAR(8),
orderMade DATETIME, orderShipped DATETIME);
```

Here's the data being inserted:

```
INSERT INTO purchases VALUES(MD5("001/Fred
Smith"),55424,"32", "34", "", NOW(), NULL);

INSERT INTO purchases VALUES(MD5("001/Bob
Jones"),55424,"36", "32", "", NOW(), NULL);

INSERT INTO purchases VALUES(MD5("002/Fred
Smith"),33212,"10.5", "", "", NOW(), NULL);

INSERT INTO purchases VALUES(MD5("002/Bob
Jones"),33212,"12.0", "", "", NOW(), NULL);
```

This produces the following table with different `nameHash` values for each entry:

nameHash	prNum	size1	size2	orderMade
6d09e7c9efe7ef8cc0dc74f8d14b0833	55424	32	34	2001-11-20 08:19:11
364af046a95dcef080db2b8e43a65397	55424	36	32	2001-11-20 08:19:11
40f3effbb6ea48909a4f40aa97f991cf	33212	10.5		2001-11-20 08:19:11
e87f6a2ccded06b9fedcc624c9ca87e8	33212	12.0		2001-11-20 08:19:11

This solution is clearly much slower. The client must calculate or list each of the values, something that can be quite slow if done interactively. It keeps asking for a new value until it receives a null answer. Then it can be sure that all the data was found. This process can be accelerated a bit by gathering the requests together with OR clauses like this:

```
SELECT * FROM purchases WHERE nameHash=MD5("001/Fred Smith")
or nameHash=MD5("002/Fred Smith");
```

The best solution depends largely on the bottlenecks in your system and the average numbers of equivalent entries. Gathering together multiple queries in this way usually makes sense unless the average number is small.

An additional layer of secrecy can be created by producing a standard series of random values or words to replace *num*. If an attacker can guess a person's name, then the attacker can add "001","002" etc. A strange sequence of values like {"koosbane41","applecart800","kepler2go",....} acts like a sequence of passwords. That level of secrecy is probably not worth the trouble.

3.8   Keeping Some Information in the Clear

There may be times when it makes sense to split the information and not pass all of it through a one-way function. A good example is a database of credit card purchases. The actual credit card number is a valuable commodity, and many clerks abused their access to such information in the past. Storing the information in a translucent database makes plenty of sense.

But the translucent database can also impede the clerks who are trying clear up mistakes. There are many times when a person may call to ask or complain about an order. If a credit card transaction fails for some reason, the clerks need a way to refer to the card itself and talk about it. One of the best solutions is to use the last four digits of the card as a surrogate for the card itself. Most people will not have two cards with the same last four digits.

The same solution works well for sensitive values like Social Security numbers or serial numbers. Blocking out all but a few digits provides translucency without damaging useability. The complete value can be stored after passing it through a one-way function. If someone presents the complete value, the result can be computed again and tested like the password example above. No clerks, however, can misuse the database to recover the value.

Here's an example of a credit card database that keeps a record of all of the successful and unsuccessful transactions:

When it is dark in the east, it is light in the west; when things are dark in the south there is still light in the north.
– Chinese Proverb

```
CREATE TABLE cc1 (orderNum INTEGER, creditcard CHAR(32),
lastFour CHAR(4), trouble BOOL, name CHAR(40));
```

The last four digits of the credit card are placed in `lastFour`, while the MD5 hash of the number is stored in `creditcard`. The name is stored in the clear, in `name` in this example, although it could also be run through MD5 to provide some privacy and security. The `orderNum` field holds the order number.

3.8.1   Inserting a Credit Card Number

Here's some basic Java code for adding a credit card value to the the `cc1` table. The function `packCCNum` removes all non-numerals from the `String` fed to the MD5 hash. This prevents any problem that might occur because of extra spaces or punctuation marks. The function `bundleTransaction` creates a `String` containing an SQL command line inserting the record. It uses the database's built-in `MD5` function to compute the value of MD5; `addTransaction` calls another class, `DatabaseWrapper`, that passes the `INSERT` over to the database. The code in `dw` uses JDBC to provide the correct passwords and gain access to the distant database:

```java
public String packCCNum(String s){
  int l=s.length();
  char c;
  StringBuffer ans=new StringBuffer();
  for (int i=0;i<l;i++){
```

```
      c=s.charAt(i);
      if ((c>='0') && (c<='9'))
        ans.append(c);
    }
    return ans.toString();
}

public String bundleTransaction(String name, int orderNum,
                                String ccNum){
    String cc=packCCNum(ccNum);
    int l=ccNum.length();
    StringBuffer ans=new StringBuffer();
    ans.append("INSERT INTO cc1 VALUES(");
    ans.append(orderNum);
    ans.append(",MD5(");
    ans.append(cc);
    ans.append("),");
    ans.append(ccNum.substring(l-4,l));
    ans.append(",0,'");
    ans.append(name);
    ans.append("');");
    System.out.println(ans.toString());
    return ans.toString();
}
public void addTransaction(String name, int orderNum, String ccNum){
    try{
      dw.executeUpdate(bundleTransaction(name,orderNum,ccNum));
    } catch (Exception e){
      System.out.println("SQL Exception:"+e);
    }
}
```

3.8.2   Using the Information

The database can be quite useful for preventing fraud and credit card abuse. If the firm has a problem with a credit card, it can flag it for the future by flipping the bit in the `trouble` field. Every new transaction can be checked against this record to look for past problems.

Here are three functions that also use the `DatabaseWrapper` to access the distant MySQL database using JDBC calls. Both `pastSuccess` and `testTrouble` receive the information in a JDBC class known as a `ResultSet`. If a credit card has been flagged, these functions will respond with a warning. If trouble appears, `signalTrouble` can be used to UPDATE a record to flag bad cards.

```
public void signalTrouble(String ccNum){
    String q="UPDATE cc1 SET trouble=1 WHERE creditcard=MD5(";
    q=q+packCCNum(ccNum)+");";
    dw.executeUpdate(q);
}

public boolean testTrouble(String ccNum){
  try{
    String q="SELECT trouble FROM cc1 WHERE creditcard=MD5(";
```

```
    q=q+packCCNum(ccNum)+");";
    ResultSet rs=dw.executeQuery(q);
    while(rs.next()){
      if (rs.getInt(1)!=0){
        return true;
      }
    }
  } catch (SQLException e){
    System.out.println("SQL Exception:"+e);
  }
    return false;
}

public boolean pastSuccess(String ccNum){
  boolean foundOne=false;
  try{
    String q="SELECT trouble FROM cc1 WHERE creditcard=MD5(";
    q=q+packCCNum(ccNum)+");";
    ResultSet rs=dw.executeQuery(q);
    while (rs.next()){
        foundOne=true;
      if (rs.getInt(1)==1){
        return false;
      }
    }
  } catch (SQLException e){
    System.out.println("SQL Exception:"+e);
  }
    return foundOne;
  }
```

Here's a snapshot of a database after five transactions are added:

orderNum	creditcard	lastFour	trouble	name
412341234	69dbac14239dbd3be2a96e83e4c98190	4432	0	Harrison Jones
443242111	69dbac14239dbd3be2a96e83e4c98190	4432	0	Harrison Jones
443244421	7f10b84c9e949f7817fd2951a4a883bd	1121	0	Cecilia Caterakis
443524241	64ca1068922c5ac29159bfae87fdd830	4122	0	Camilia Anderson
443524223	5541955cc01444368e502b27e5da553e	2114	1	Sarah Bande

3.9 Conclusions

One-way functions are powerful tools for obscuring information from prying eyes. They scramble data while still making it possible to use the data in some reasonable ways. This chapter showed how to build several simple databases for protecting store purchase information or salary data from people who might misuse their access to the databases. In the examples, the curious may be able to discover that someone bought a particular pair of pants, but they won't know who. Snoops might discover that someone made $122,300 last year, but they won't know who. The legitimate users, though, will be able to use all of the functions of the database.

The translucency guarantees are far from perfect. In the first example in Section 3.1, anyone who knows a person's name can look up the information. The database responds to all calls with $h(name)$ in it.

3.9.1   Lessons

- Additional information can be mixed into the one-way function to add more security. Using a one-way function like $h(name/address)$ requires a person to know the name *and* the address to look up information.

- Adding a secret password ($h(name/password)$) adds more security.

- The one problem with using one-way functions like this is their perfection. If they are truly irreversible, then the results from $h(\text{"}Michael\text{"})$, $h(\text{"}Mike\text{"})$, $h(\text{"}MIKE\text{"})$ and $h(\text{"}mike\text{"})$ will be very different. That feature can turn into a bug if a user mistypes something.

- The easiest way to defend against this problem is to reduce the input into a canonical form free from strange characters, spaces and punctuation. Converting each string into either uppercase or lowercase reduces the risk of typographical errors even further.

- Reducing the number of allowable characters also reduces the security by making it easier for someone to step through all different combinations. Ideally, this canonical form will still offer enough security because the number of characters allowed will still be large enough to prevent someone from testing all possible combinations.

- Added flexibility and forgiveness can be factored into the mix by adding additional columns to the database. If the identification value is computed by using a one-way function on fields A, B, C and D, then each entry in the database may include $h(A/B/C/D)$, $h(A/B/C)$, $h(A/B/D)$, $h(A/C/D)$, and $h(B/C/D)$.

- Chapter 5 shows how to use one-way functions to synchronize the schedules of two or more people.

- Standard software packages can create canonical forms. Section 10.2 uses the Java `Date` classes for dates and times.

Chapter 4

Coordinating Users

The examples in Chapter 3 show how to create basic translucent databases with one mechanism for retrieving the data. The information in the table is indexed with $h(info)$. Anyone who knows $info$ gets the rest of the row back. The information acts like a key.

Sometimes it makes sense to add extra keys to the mixture to create additional layers of accessibility or secrecy. People who know one key may not know the other, but the database can control access by delivering the right information to the people who know the right keys.

Translucent databases provide this access control without all the extra mechanisms. Many databases have one section of the code for retrieving information and another for section ensuring that a person has the right to retrieve that information. The databases generally do a good job delivering what they promise, but the complexity and the overhead can be substantial. Translucent databases offer a simpler solution that allows database designers to concentrate on offering faster retrieval. The access control comes free.

The mechanism here is simple. If you know the right key, you get access to the information. Some information needs multiple keys. Some requires any one of a handful of keys. Any strange combination of keys can be created by adding more columns to the table and filling these columns with the results of hashing different sets of keys.

This approach is not without limits. Much of the complexity from the access control mechanism is shifted to the problem of juggling all the keys. Each user doesn't have just one login name and one password anymore.

The translucent databases also lack central control. A database administrator cannot grant privileges one day, take them away for a few weeks and then grant them again. The data is more in the control of the individual users, not the central administrator.

Some databases call for central control and can't use all the schemes in this chapter. It would be terrible for a business if the ability to edit the salary information could not be turned on and off. The list of people with the ability to alter the amount of money in a bank account should be flexible because the power should not last for a lifetime.

But these limits come with advantages. Lack of control means lack of responsibility. The translucent databases in this chapter don't need heavy security, and they don't fail dramatically if someone hacks around the security system. The data is stored in a way that no one can get access, not even the most powerful system administrator with root-level power.

The limitations are also not as great as they may seem. Passwords can be handed down from one person to another. If one person gets access to the data, another one doesn't need to lose it.

4.1   A Bulletin Board Example

Many conferences, campgrounds, and other gathering sites have bulletin boards where people can post notes for friends. The mechanism was an important way for meeting people at large gatherings in the days before cellphones and wireless email.

This mechanism simulates a bulletin board where two people can exchange notes with a simple database. The table contains three columns: one for the sender's name, one for the recipient's name and one for the message:

```
CREATE TABLE bboard1 (nameHash1 CHAR(32),nameHash2 CHAR(32),
message BLOB);
```

The names are stored after passing them through a one-way function. The message can be any pile of bits, including an image or a sound file:

```
INTO bboard1 VALUES(MD5("Ricky"),MD5("Lucy"),"You've got
some explaining to do.");
```

```
INSERT INTO bboard1 VALUES(MD5("Lucy"), MD5("Ricky"), "It's
not my fault.");
```

Producing this table

nameHash1	nameHash2	message
0860cf806314c1f1ea14aaf90bc98e08	80eb0e612760f756547b660c4c71ba7d	You've got some explaining to do.
80eb0e612760f756547b660c4c71ba7d	0860cf806314c1f1ea14aaf90bc98e08	It's not my fault.

People can recover the messages addressed to themselves with one line:

```
SELECT * FROM bboard1 WHERE nameHash2=MD5("Ricky");
```

4.1.1   Adding a Shared Password

The messages can also be encrypted by using a shared password known by both of them:

```
INSERT INTO bboard1 VALUES(MD5("Lucy"), MD5("Ricky"),
ENCODE("Where are you?","Little Ricky"));
```

The phrase "Little Ricky" acts as the password.

The value does not need to be an agreed upon in advance. It could simply be derived from their names:

```
INSERT INTO bboard1 VALUES(MD5("Lucy"), MD5("Ricky"),
ENCODE("Where are you?","Lucy/Ricky"));
```

The password is the sender's name concatenated with the recipient's. That system avoids the problem of deciding upon a secret password in advance, but it forces the recipient to guess the name (and the spelling) of the person who sent the message. All the techniques from Section 3.2 can help by removing extra spaces and punctuation, but finding the right name cannot be easy.

A simpler solution is just to use the recipient's name as the password:

```
INSERT INTO bboard1 VALUES(MD5("Lucy"), MD5("Ricky"),
ENCODE("Where are you?","Ricky"));
```

In all these cases, the password adds some additional security that keeps the information out of the hands of the browsers with the greatest amount of access.

4.2 Special One-Way Functions

For most operations in this book, all the one-way function behave in the same way. The $h(x)$ function scrambles x until it is not recognizable. If you change the order you feed items into h, change their spelling, or change their punctuation, then everything comes out in a different form. The output is very dependent on the order of the input.

The one-way function created by raising a number to a power modulo a prime number has all these features *and* the ability to separate and re-order the input. If $h(x) = g^x \bmod p$, then $h(x)h(y) = g^x g^y \bmod p = g^{x+y} \bmod p$. The values of $h(x + y)$ can be computed in two parts as $g^x \bmod p$ and $g^y \bmod p$. That can be an advantage if the owner of x or y doesn't want to reveal this information to another.

The parts can also be separated using the now classical trick used by Whitfield Diffie and Martin Hellman as one of the first examples of public-key cryptography. [DH76a, DH76b, DH77] The value of $g^{xy} \bmod p$ can be computed in two steps. First, the owner of the value x computes $g^x \bmod p$. Then, the other person raises that value to the y power: $(g^x \bmod p)^y \bmod p$. This value can also be computed in the other order: $(g^x \bmod p)^y \bmod p = (g^y \bmod p)^x \bmod p = g^{xy} \bmod p$.

Chapter 11 uses this feature to build an inscrutible accounting system.

Separating the computation of a number like that can be quite valuable in many situations in which two people don't trust each other but must cooperate. Section 7.3 describes one situation where control of information must be shared between two or more people.

The rest of this section describes another version of the bulletin board created in Section 4.1. It imitates public-key encryption to scramble the message passed between two people.

4.2.1   Creating A Public Key

In this example, there are two tables. The first table holds each user's public key. That is, a value of g chosen at random, a prime number, p, also chosen at random, and the value $g^x \bmod p$. Each person keeps the value of x secret. The second table holds the messages.

Here's the SQL code for creating the first table:

```
CREATE TABLE pubkeys (name TINYTEXT, gee TINYTEXT, geex
TINYTEXT, pea TINYTEXT);
```

I chose to store these as text values to make debugging a bit easier. The TINYTEXT columns in MySQL hold between 0 to 255 characters and use another byte to specify their length. You may want to leave the information in binary form to make things a bit faster. This mechanism can be made faster and more efficient by choosing a fixed value of p and limiting the size of the columns. The values g, p and $g^x \bmod p$ will not be longer than this fixed p.

The same pubkeys *table is used in Section 10.2.2 to create digital signatures for entries in the table.*
This Java code for the function insertPublicKey creates a public key and inserts it into the database. The corresponding private key, x, is generated by hashing a password using an implementation of MD5. The value of p is chosen at random using Java's built-in BigInteger class. The value of g is also created at random. Both of these use another value chosen from the results of further hashing of the passphrase, using the MD5Bean.

This hashing uses random phrases I picked to scramble the value with more complexity: "Translucent Databases rock." and "Translucent Databases really rock." They add a small amount of security by making it difficult for an attacker to duplicate the calculations. The phrases themselves can't be kept truly secret, but they can be embedded in the compiled code where they may not be easily found. If, for example, you're creating your own version which won't need to interact with mine, you should change the phrases. You can also use different phrases in different distinct implementations. Most of the security, though, comes from the user's choice of a passphrase.

```
public String insertPublicKey(String nm, String passphrase){
    // construct value of x from passphrase.
    MD5Bean.clear();
    MD5Bean.Update("Translucent Databases rock.");
    MD5Bean.Update(passphrase);
    byte[] hashedPass=MD5Bean.Final();
    BigInteger x=new BigInteger(hashedPass);
```

```
    // construct prime number.
    MD5Bean.Update("Translucent Databases really rock.");
    MD5Bean.Update(passphrase);
    Random seed=new Random(MD5Bean.getMD5State().getStateInt(0));
    BigInteger p=new BigInteger(768, 5, seed );

    // construct generator.
    MD5Bean.Update("More hype? Nah.");
    MD5Bean.Update(passphrase);
    seed=new Random(MD5Bean.getMD5State().getStateInt(0));
     BigInteger g=new BigInteger(760, 5, seed );

    // calculate value.
    BigInteger geex=g.modPow(x,p);

    //create query.
    StringBuffer query=new StringBuffer("INSERT INTO pubkeys VALUES('");
    query.append(nm);
    query.append("','");
    query.append(g.toString());
    query.append("','");
    query.append(geex.toString());
    query.append("','");
    query.append(p.toString());
    query.append("');");


    System.out.println("query="+query);
    return query.toString();
}
```

This current implementation is entirely deterministic. If you run the algorithm with the same value of passphrase, you'll get the same key. That can be useful if the database table pubkeys is not always available to the recipient. Users can regenerate their keys whenever called for. Changing the choice of Random to be more random will fix that.

Here's an abbreviated version of the query produced from the parameters "Harrison Jones" and "tomatoes":

```
    INSERT INTO pubkeys VALUES('Harrison Jones',
    '3113931...','147186041...','797166508614...');
```

4.2.2 Using the Public Key

The one-way functions can use the information from the public-key table, pubkeys, to scramble messages intended for particular people. Only the ones who know the right passphrase can recover it. Anyone can send these messages or store data for a particular person without knowing the person's passphrase. That makes an ideal tool for allowing two (or more) people to synchronize their plans and information while keeping the database translucent.

Here's the SQL command creating the table:

```
CREATE TABLE messages (toName TINYTEXT, fromName TINYTEXT, m
BLOB, geey TINYTEXT);
```

This example uses a simple table that stores the message in one column, `m`, that could hold any amount of information. This `BLOB` is a block of bytes used by the built-in encryption function, `ENCODE`, of MySQL. This example uses the built-in function for simplicity. If you want more security, you could handle all the encryption at the client, perhaps with a Java applet. The message travels in the clear in this example:

The sender (`fromName`) and the recipient (`toName`) are also left in the clear in this example. They could easily be passed through a one-way function for some additional security. The advantage of that step, though, would be minimal because the public-key table, `pubkeys`, must hold each person's name in the clear. How else would anyone look up the public key of another? If all the names are available, they could be used to find the information awaiting each person in `messages` by going through the names one by one. That is, for every name found by executing a `SELECT name FROM pubkeys`, execute the command `SELECT m FROM messages WHERE toName=MD5(name)`. The value of MD5 adds little here so it's left out. The information is still secure, though, because it has been encrypted.

The column `geey` holds the value $g^y \bmod p$, where y is a random value chosen to scramble the message. The sender begins by looking up $g^x \bmod p$, g, and p from the public-key table. The value of $g^{xy} \bmod p$ is computed from $(g^x \bmod p)^y \bmod p$. Remember that raising a value to a power modulo a prime is a one-way function. Anyone who gains access to the public-key database can't use this information to figure out x. That will be important in the next section because only the person who holds the value of x will be able to use the information stored in the table `messages`. The information in the table `pubkeys` won't be enough to decode the messages.

Sometimes $h(g^{xy} \bmod p)$ is more secure if h is a hash function like SHA. Generic hash functions destroy algebraic properties that might be exploited by an attacker.

This value of $g^{xy} \bmod p$ is converted into a shorter key by using the MD5Bean to hash the value. This extra security is not necessary, but it is a simple way to build a shorter key that still depends upon all the digits of $g^{xy} \bmod p$. The code is already written, so why not just use it as a quick shortening tool. That value is passed as a hexadecimal string to the built-in MySQL DECODE function.

Here's the Java code:

```
public void insertMessage(String from, String to,
                          String message){
   String findQuery="SELECT * FROM pubkeys WHERE name='"+to+"'";;
   try{
     ResultSet rs=dw.executeQuery(findQuery);
     rs.next(); // get the first match.

     String gee=rs.getString("gee");
     String pea=rs.getString("pea");
     String geex=rs.getString("geex");

     BigInteger gx=new BigInteger(geex);
```

```
BigInteger p=new BigInteger(pea);
BigInteger y=new BigInteger(760,5,new Random());
BigInteger g=new BigInteger(gee);
BigInteger gy=g.modPow(y,p);

// Compute secret key.
BigInteger key=gx.modPow(y,p);
MD5Bean.clear();
MD5Bean.Update(key.toByteArray());

// Construct query.
StringBuffer query=new StringBuffer();
query.append("INSERT INTO messages VALUES('");
query.append(to);
query.append("','");
query.append(from);
query.append("',ENCODE('");
query.append(message);
query.append("','");
query.append(MD5Bean.asHex());
query.append("'),'");
query.append(gy.toString());
query.append("')";);

dw.executeQuery(query.toString());
System.out.println(query);
} catch (java.sql.SQLException e){

}

}
```

Here's a sample query produced by the code:

```
INSERT INTO messages VALUES('Harrison Jones','Fred Jones',
ENCODE('Hello Harry','c72a36df8ab0f70e3e2488c4ed89a364'),
'611207057644657489328348900912358930163816365...');
```

4.2.3 Recovering Messages

Recovering the messages is very similar to encoding them. The key for scrambling the message is still created by finding $g^{xy} \bmod p$. In this case, though, the receiver must use $g^y \bmod p$ stored with the message itself.

Once the sender destroys the value of y, the only way to decrypt the message is to know x. The information in the public-key table, pubkeys, isn't of any value. It holds $g^x \bmod p$. But there is no known way to take $g^x \bmod p$ and $g^y \bmod p$ and merge them to produce $g^{xy} \bmod p$. You can produce $g^{x+y} \bmod p$ by multiplying them and $g^{x-y} \bmod p$ by dividing one by the other, but you can't get $g^{xy} \bmod p$ without knowing either x or y.

The value of x is reconstructed by passing the value of the passphrase through the MD5Bean one-way function again. The value of $g^y \bmod p$ is recovered from the messages table, and the value of p is recovered from the pubkeys table. The value $g^{xy} \bmod p$ is computed from that information and then passed, once more, through the MD5Bean to shorten it.

For the sake of simplicity, this code tries to recover only the first messages sent to a particular person. A more sophisticated version will decode each value returned by the ResultSet in turn. This is actually easier if the encryption is done locally at the client because using the DECODE function in MySQL requires another query to the database itself.

Here's the function recoverMessages:

```
public void recoverMessages(String nm, String passphrase){
    MD5Bean.clear();
    MD5Bean.Update("Translucent Databases rock.") ;
    MD5Bean.Update(passphrase);
    byte[] hashedPass=MD5Bean.Final();
    BigInteger x=new BigInteger(hashedPass);

    String findQuery="SELECT * FROM messages WHERE toName='";
    findQuery=findQuery+nm+"'";;

    String findPeaQuery="SELECT * FROM pubkeys WHERE name='";
    findPeaQuery=findPeaQuery+nm+"'";;

    try{
      // find the prime number.
      ResultSet rsp=dw.executeQuery(findPeaQuery);
      rsp.next();// the first public key.
      String pea=rsp.getString("pea");
      BigInteger p=new BigInteger(pea);


      ResultSet rs=dw.executeQuery(findQuery);
      rs.next(); // get the first match.

      // compute key
      String geey=rs.getString("geey");
      BigInteger gy=new BigInteger(geey);
      BigInteger key=gy.modPow(x,p);
      MD5Bean.clear();
      MD5Bean.Update(key.toByteArray());


      // Blob =rs.getBlob("m");
      // use this to decode the data locally.
      // or
      String query="SELECT DECODE(m,'";
      query=query+ MD5Bean.asHex()+"') FROM messages";;
      ResultSet rs2=dw.executeQuery(query);
      rs2.next();// get the first row only here.
      System.out.println(rs2.getString(1));

    } catch (java.sql.SQLException e){

    }

}
```

Running that function with the two parameters `"Harrison Jones"` and `"tomatoes"` produces the message, "Hello Harry".

4.2.4   Using Public-Key One-Way Functions

The three Java functions in Sections 4.2.1 through 4.2.3 show how simple code can create complex translucent databases. The information in the table `messages` can't be understood by anyone who breaks into the database. The clerks can't understand it, the management can't understand it, and the hackers can't understand it. If the encryption is done at the applet, then eavesdroppers can't understand the message either. Yet the database serves as a simple way for two people to send messages to each other.

Passing messages is a primitive metaphor for a technique that can be used in many different ways. The solutions provide a way to create locked drop boxes for information. Data comes into the table, but only the person with the right `passphrase` can recover it.

Here are some places where it might be valuable:

Complaint Box Anyone can file information in the database, but only the boss who holds the right `passphrase` can recover the information.

Benefit Notices Did the insurance company reject your claim for treatment? No one needs to know but you. Storing personal records in a database with this technique locks out everyone else.

Section 7.3 shows a more powerful algorithm for a suggestion box that requires two or more people to read the messages.

Local Information Not every client or every person can maintain a secure server where information can travel. This solution provides a simple way to give clients or partners their own local places to recover data. Imagine, for instance, that you often buy some commodity from several different vendors. To keep an upper hand, you don't show the amount you order from each supplier to another supplier. A database built with this mechanism could hold the orders destined for each supplier in private. Each supplier could read only its own messages. A more complicated database granting privileges to each supplier could serve the same purpose, but this mechanism is simpler and easier to implement.

Object Message Databases In some of the most progressive architectures, the programmers create plug-ins that work within a larger application, like a database, a typesetting program or browser. In these cases, the plug-in can't trust the application, and vice versa. The application controls the plug-in by limiting communications to predetermined channels. The plug-in can use techniques like these to protect communications from the application at large. The technique is not perfect because the plug-in's memory can be viewed by others, but it offers some protection.

4.3   Conclusion

Sometimes two or more people need to cooperate to synchronize information. Chapter 5 uses basic hash functions to let people set schedules. This chapter describes how to use the techniques to pass messages. The first examples use basic hash functions, but the later ones use some of the more convenient public-key encryption solutions.

Many examples in this chapter aren't very complicated. The applications store encrypted information instead of unencrypted information. Carefully choosing the password makes it possible for multiple people to use the same database. Chapter 5 uses more complex versions of these algorithms to provide more complicated access.

4.3.1   Lessons

- Two people can work together with a database if both keep shared secrets, a and b, and use them to make a password for encrypting information with a one-way function, $h(ab)$.

- All the algorithms in this chapter can be generalized to work with more than two people.

- If basic one-way functions like cryptographically secure hash functions are used, then everyone needs to know the secrets.

- In low-security applications, the "secrets" may just be public information, like a name. A bulletin board at a conference, for instance, may exchange messages between people using just the names as the secrets. The increased convenience may be worth the relative insecurity because many attendees are anonymous to one another.

- Public-key approaches can add security. One person can store information for another, but only the other can read the information.

Chapter 5

Synchronization

Many databases act as tools for two or more people to synchronize their schedules. At first glance, protecting the information *and* letting several people use the data seems difficult or perhaps impossible. If two people work together, they need to exchange information.

This chapter explores the topic by building several tools to allow a group of baby sitters and a group of parents to coordinate their schedules. Every parent knows that finding a baby sitter who is free is a tough job. First, you call one who eventually returns the call to beg off because of a big party. The second one takes a day to return the call because of basketball practice. That goes on and on until someone accepts the job. Email can speed this task up a bit because the search is inherently serial. One person can't be offered the job until another declines. This basic problem confounds parents and, for that matter, anyone who needs to synchronize schedules.

The translucent databases used as examples in this chapter store the schedules of baby sitters. This information must be treated with care because it contains the whereabouts of minors. It might be used by someone looking for a house without parents to burglarize or maybe by someone with even more sinister intentions. Locking the information in a translucent database prevents even the best hackers, eavesdroppers or system administrators from nabbing the data.

This approach may even make such a service possible. baby sitting is not a lucrative job, so baby sitters are unlikely to pay much for the scheduling service. Storing translucent data in a cheap database with basic security can greatly reduce the costs of providing the service. Spending a few minutes to implement the technique with a translucent database makes it possible to run the system on a cheap shared server without the high upkeep of a secure, guarded system.

The chapter explores several approaches to the solution, beginning with the simplest and ending with the most complicated.

5.1   The Baby Sitter's Table

The simplest solution is not much different from the database of past purchases from a department store discussed in Section 3.1. Each baby sitter begins with one password, p_a, which can be distributed to each parent who may want to hire the baby sitter. Anyone who knows that password can dig up the sitter's schedule.

Here's the SQL command for creating the basic table:

```
CREATE TABLE babysitter1 (idHash CHAR(32), description
TINYTEXT, free TINYINT, eventType TINYINT, eventStart
DATETIME, eventEnd DATETIME);
```

The `idHash` contains the MD5 hash of the sitter's name and password, $h(name, p_a)$, concatenated together. A short explanation of the event is stored in `description`. The boolean value `free` is set to be true (1) if the baby sitter is free and ready to go. If it is false (0), the event represents a time when the baby sitter is busy and can't be booked.

Chapter 12 describes more complex tricks played with exponentiation-based one-way functions.

The starting and ending times are stored in SQL's internal format as `eventStart` and `eventEnd`. The event itself is encoded as the integer `eventType`. Some suggested values are:

1 One time only, beginning at `eventStart` and ending at `eventEnd`.

2 Once a month on the same numbered day as `eventStart`.

3 Once a month on the same relative day as `eventStart`. So if `eventStart` is designated as the second Tuesday, then this event will always occur on the second Tuesday.

4 Once a week on the same day as `eventStart`.

5 Every weekday at the times specified in `eventStart` and `eventEnd`.

6 Every weekend at the times specified in `eventStart` and `eventEnd`.

7 Every year on the same day and time in `eventStart` and `eventEnd`.

An event is created and stored with a command like this:

```
INSERT INTO babysitter1 VALUES(MD5("Chris Jones/swordfish"),
"New Year's Party All Night Long", 0,1,"2000-12-31
20:00:00","2001-01-01 20:00:00");
```

This means that the baby sitter won't be available from 8 pm on New Year's eve until 8 pm the following day.

Any parent interested in hiring Chris Jones can type the name and password into a SELECT command like this:

```
SELECT * FROM babysitter1 WHERE idHash=MD5("Chris
Jones/swordfish");
```

In practice, a complicated command like that should use either a servlet, some Perl code, some PHP or maybe an applet to interpret the results and display them.

5.2 Adding More Names

The example in Section 5.1 offers some basic control to the baby sitter. Only someone who knows a sitter's name and password can look up that sitter's schedule. Everyone else is locked out.

This all-or-nothing approach can be useful, but it has limits. If the relationship between a sitter and some parents sours, the sitter can't lock out individuals. The only solution is to change the name or password and then tell only the acceptable parents the new pasword. Everyone is inconvenienced.

Another solution is to store multiple copies of the schedule under different name and password combinations. One set of parents may be told the password "swordfish" while another set learns the password "sea bass". The software interface between the baby sitter and the database can automatically insert the record multiple times:

```
INSERT INTO babysitter1 VALUES(MD5("Chris Jones/swordfish"),
"No practice and no school.", 1,1,"2001-01-02
16:00:00","2001-01-02 23:00:00");

INSERT INTO babysitter1 VALUES(MD5("Chris Jones/sea bass"),
"No practice and no school.", 1,1,"2001-01-02
16:00:00","2001-01-02 23:00:00");
```

The software shell around the database can be as simple or as complicated as needed. A simple one could routinely add all events to the database using all name and password combinations. When one set of parents is excluded, no new events are added using that combination. One command could delete all rows where idHash=MD5("Chris Jones/swordfish") if called for.

A more complicated version could juggle the schedules, allowing a baby sitter to project different information to different customers. The extra complexity may not be worth it to many users. It may be more useful in other situations where people are more duplicitous or where information is more tightly circulated on a need-to-know basis.

One might compare the journey of the soul to mystical union, by way of pure faith, to the journey of a car on a dark highway. The only way the driver can keep to the road is by using his headlights.
–Thomas Merton
Reason in the Life of Contemplation

5.3 Multiple Tables

Adding multiple entries for each set of parents is a simple solution, but ultimately a wasteful one. Copying data may not cost much with today's gigabyte disks, but inefficiency is never a good policy. The solution in Section 5.2 is also not very secure. Every parent knows the name and password combination. They can log in and change the schedule if necessary.

A better solution for both of these problems is to create another password, p_s, available only to the sitter. The parents' names and optional passwords are stored in a separate table. The events are still stored in a table like babysitter1, containing a list of events matched with an idHash, but this time idHash is set to be $h(name, p_s)$, the hash of the name and the secret password, "porterhouse5".

```
INSERT INTO babysitter1 VALUES(MD5("Chris
Jones/porterhouse5"), "School play auditions.",
0,1,"2001-01-08 14:30:00","2001-01-08 19:00:00");
```

No one except the baby sitter knows that password.

The names of the parents with access to a baby sitter's schedule are stored in a separate database:

```
CREATE TABLE parents1 (idHash CHAR(32), parentHash
CHAR(32));
```

The first column, idHash, contains the same one-way function applied to a sitter's name and secret password: $h(name, p_s)$. The second column, parentHash, contains the parent's name and optional password, after they are passed through a one-way function:

```
INSERT INTO parents1 VALUES(MD5("Chris Jones/porterhouse5"),
MD5("Kate and Steve Homeland/pizza5"));
```

The extra password, p_k = "*pizza5*", is optional. It may not be important for many applications. Some packages may implement it by using the same password for all parents just to add another layer of security. The security it adds is limited here because every baby sitter must know p_k to add a parent to the sitter's list. Its chief job is to keep interlopers from typing in names alone.

A more complicated version would use a password chosen by the parents and given to the sitter, a system that would give the parent some control. Of course, the sitter would need to know the parent's password to add the parent to the database or change the parent's entry.

Separating the event and parental access information into two columns avoids duplication and adds some security. When a parent searches for available sitters, the software shell searches in two steps with one MATCH:

1. All matches with the right value of parentHash are found int the parents1 table:

   ```
   SELECT idHash FROM parents1 WHERE parentHash=MD5("Kate
   and Steve Homeland/pizza5");
   ```

2. Then all records from `babysitter1` are found with the same value(s) of `idHash`. If several baby sitters place the parents on the list, then all of the events for these baby sitters will appear.

This search can be combined into a `JOIN` command:

```
SELECT description,free,eventType,eventStart,eventEnd FROM
parents1,babysitter1 WHERE
parents1.idHash=babysitter1.idHash AND
parents1.parentHash=MD5("Kate and Steve Homeland/pizza5");
```

Produces:

School play auditions. 0   1   2001-01-08 14:30:00   2001-01-08 19:00:00

Tuning this `JOIN` for your database can yield faster results.

In this example, the column `parentHash` is scrambled to add an extra level of security. Idle browsers can't spot parents' names and look for the `idHash` values matched with them. That extra information may be useful to an attacker.

Not all implementations or applications need that amount of security. The names of the parents could be left in the clear to allow browsers to find their names. If baby sitters are adding the names of their customers, they may not type the names in the same way that the customers type them. The chummy Mom who tells the sitter, "Just call me Kate," may always spell out the name "Catherine" when filling out forms. Names also have many homonyms. Names like Caroline and Catherine, for instance, may have dozens of relatively standard spellings. If this column is left in the clear, customers can browse the column.

Splitting the database in tht way adds more security and efficiency. Baby sitters can add and drop parents without duplicating or eliminating many rows of the database. Parents have just as much access as they need, but they don't know the name and password the baby sitter uses to add information. That is more secure because it prevents parents from adding new events in the baby sitter's name by using their knowledge of the password, p_a. They can't use the standard software shell to generate spurious events, maybe to block out other parents.

5.4 Adding Extra Information

The example in Section 5.3 shows how to split the database into two tables to provide more efficiency and security. That approach keeps the parents away from the baby sitter's password, p_s, but it creates another problem. Parents searching the database won't know the baby sitter associated with each record recovered. If parents find themselves on the approved lists of multiple baby

sitters, all the events for these baby sitters will appear after the search, and
there will be no way to tell them apart.

One simple way solution is to add another column with the baby sitter's
name:

```
CREATE TABLE babysitter2 (idHash CHAR(32), name BLOB,
description TINYTEXT, free TINYINT, eventType TINYINT,
eventStart DATETIME, eventEnd DATETIME);
```

That makes it possible to determine just who is going to audition for the
school play. Of course, that also breaks the veil of translucency by putting the
baby sitter's name on every event the sitter enters into the database.

This transparency can be eliminated by encrypting the information on
this column with a password. Call this p_m, a password to encrypt any message carried in the record. This Java code generates a unique password, p_m,
by passing the baby sitter's name and regular secret password, p_s through a
one-way function. We can't reuse the baby sitter's regular password, p_s, because the password, p_m, needs to be shared with parents so they can decode
the information.

Here's some Java code to create the password:

```
public String generatePrivatePassword(String name,
                                       String password){
  MD5Bean.clear();
  MD5Bean.Update("A set phrase for extra security.") ;
  MD5Bean.Update(name+password);
  return MD5Bean.asHex();
}

public String scrambleName(String name,
                           String password){
  String ans="ENCODE('"+name+"','";
  ans=ans+generatePrivatePassword(name,password)+"')";
  return ans;
}
```

That code produces a phrase that can be inserted into the SQL query for
a MySQL database. This particular version uses the built-in ENCODE function,
but it could also use a local encryption version.

This password, p_m, does not reveal the baby sitter's secret password, p_s because it comes from hashing the secret password and the baby sitter's name.
An attacker may know the baby sitter's name, but p_s can only be found by list-
ing all possible values, hashing them together with the name, and then testing
to see if the result equals p_m.

Executing scrambleName(String name, String password) produces the
result that can be merged with the rest of the information:

```
INSERT INTO babysitter2 VALUES(MD5("Chris
Jones/porterhouse5"), ENCODE('Chris
Jones','bf3fd17fa5b205ca3024a85228e26b6f'), "School play
```

```
auditions.", 0,1,"2001-01-08 14:30:00","2001-01-08
19:00:00");
```

The password, p_m, is bf3fd17fa5b205ca3024a85228e26b6f. This needs to be shared with the parents so they can DECODE the results in column name. The simplest way to get that to the parents is to store the information in the parents' table, parents2:

```
CREATE TABLE parents2 (idHash CHAR(32), parentHash CHAR(32),
infoKey BLOB);
```

The field infoKey stores the value of p_s encrypted with yet another password, p_p, found from the same information used to compute parentHash.

Here's some Java code that creates the INSERT command for adding a new parent to the parent2 table:

```
public String scrambleAll(String sitterName,
                          String sitterPassword,
                          String parentName,
                          String parentPassword){

  StringBuffer ans=new StringBuffer();
  ans.append("INSERT INTO parents2 VALUES(");
   // idHash
  ans.append("MD5('");
  ans.append(sitterName);
  ans.append('/'); // not needed.
  ans.append(sitterPassword);
  ans.append("'),");
  // parentHash
  ans.append("MD5('");
  ans.append(parentName);
  ans.append('/'); // not needed.
  ans.append(parentPassword);
  ans.append("'),");

  // Include password for message decoding.
  String messagePassword=generatePrivatePassword(sitterName,
                                                  sitterPassword);

  ans.append("ENCODE('");
  ans.append(messagePassword);
  ans.append("','");
  ans.append(generatePrivatePassword(parentName,parentPassword));
  ans.append("'));");

  return ans.toString();
}
```

Executing the Java method call:
```
    scrambleAll("Chris Jones","swordfish","Kate and Steve
Homeland" ,"pizza5")
```
produces this SQL line:

```
INSERT INTO parents2 VALUES(MD5('Chris Jones/swordfish'),
MD5('Kate and Steve Homeland/pizza5'),
ENCODE('bf3fd17fa5b205ca3024a85228e26b6f',
'5909885bd7df1ceb32b309de0448ed61'));
```

The first entry is the one-way function applied to the sitter's name and password. It is stored in idHash for matching later with idHash values in the babysitter2 table. The second value is the MD5 hash of each parent's name and password so the parents can find their baby sitters later. The third value is the message password, $p_m = bf3fd17fa5b205ca3024a85228e2b6f$, encrypted with the parent's password, $p_p = 5909885bd7df1ceb32b309de0448ed61$. This is used so the parent can recover the extra information included with each event entry.

Here's a step-by-step description of what happens when Kate Homeland wants to see which baby sitters are available:

1. Kate types in her name and password: "Kate and Steve Homeland" and "pizza5". (You may choose to leave off the password from this to make the system more flexible.)

2. The software finds the parental encryption password, p_p, derived from this information using the function generatePrivatePassword("Kate and Steve Homeland","pizza5"). This is the value: 5909885bd7df-1ceb32b309de0448ed61.

3. The software shell finds all entries in parents2 where a baby sitter opens up the schedule to Kate:

   ```
   SELECT
   idHash,DECODE(infoKey,'5909885bd7df1ceb32b309de0448ed61'
   FROM parents2 WHERE parentHash=MD5('Kate and Steve
   Homeland/pizza5');
   ```

4. The parent2 table responds with one entry with the information:

   idHash=9af2e20aab17caea825525588ca2f3a4

   DECODE(infoKey,'5909885bd7df1ceb32b309de0448ed61')= bf3fd17fa5b205ca3024a85228e26b6f

5. The software uses the value from idHash to do a JOIN with the babysitter2 table.

6. The software uses the DECODEd version of infoKey to DECODE the value stored in the babysitter2 field name.

7. Kate can now see that Chris will be going to play auditions on January 8th between 2:30 pm and 7:00 pm.

This translucent database can defy a number of different attacks. The baby sitter's information is stored in a table, but no one can see the schedule without the baby sitter's permission. Each event is stored under the idHash entry and that value is computed by passing the baby sitter's name and secret password, p_s, through a one-way function. Only the baby sitter can add new events to the babysitter2 table because only the baby sitter should know p_s. That implementation uses the MD5 function built into the database for illustrative purposes, but a more secure version will compute this value on the sitter's machine.

The parents2 table controls who has access to the baby sitter's schedule. Only the parents who type in their names and passwords can recover the right values of idHash to JOIN with babysitter2. That also allows them to recover the value of p_m used to scramble the sitter's name stored in name. This could also include other information. All the data from the other columns, like eventStart or eventEnd, could also be encrypted with that password. The database designer may choose to encrypt everything to add even more security, but that impulse may be checked to increase efficiency. The JOIN process may include extra clauses that limit the search to particular days. If eventStart or eventEnd are encrypted, the SQL database can't limit the number of events found. The information must be done by the software shell itself.

The number of passwords in this mix looks daunting. There are four passwords in this description, p_s, p_m, p_p and p_k, but only two of them are known to humans. The p_m password is derived from p_s and p_p is derived from p_k. The humans need to remember only p_s and p_k. Arranging the passwords in this function adds another layer of security. The parents (or the software on the parents' machine) must learn p_m to decrypt the extra information attached to each event in babysitter2. If this value were the same as p_s, then the parents would be able to masquerade as the baby sitter. The derivation process ensures that it's not possible to figure out p_m from p_m.

If necessary, the value of p_k can be left out of the loop. The baby sitters can add parents without learning some parental password. One compromise is to let the parents choose a nickname or handle. Instead of inserting their names and passwords, p_k, they can just use generic names like, "Manhattan42", "KAG73" or "LikeICare"[1].

5.5 Security

The systems described in this chapter are generally as secure as they seem. If the one-way functions are as strong as we assume, there is no way to take the information in the database and figure out who placed what entry in the table. If the description field on one entry in babysitter2 says one sitter is busy with "hosting a slumber party", there is no way someone can take the information in idHash and crash the party.

---

[1] The best AOL login I've ever seen.

The passwords also keep browsers from poking around the database. You can't pretend to be Chris Jones or Kate Homeland without knowing their passwords.

This security is not absolute. Imagine that a pair of parents is desperate to get Chris to baby sit on Saturday night. Their child won't go to sleep for anyone else. To block Kate Homeland, they conspire to insert a fake record proclaiming that Chris will be busy all evening "carrying on, abusing substances, trashing the family's good name and generally exceeding every one of society's boundaries that can be located in such an inebriated condition." Such an entry in the `description` field could scare away other parents like Kate Homeland for good.

If the evil parents try to insert this value through the software shell wrapped around the database, they will fail unless they know Chris's password. It would be impossible to generate a fake entry for `idHash` without knowing that password. They also wouldn't know the value of p_m to hide the information in the column `name`.

If the evil parents are more nefarious, they might gain access to the database itself. They might not know the password, but they could still copy another one of Chris's entries and change the times. The problem is finding Chris's entries. If the evil parents are on Chris's list of approved parents, then they can figure out the value of `idHash` associated with Chris. Then they can take a random entry and change the times.

The doctor should be opaque to his patients and, like a mirror, should show them nothing but what is shown to him.
–Sigmund Freud Recommendations to Physicians Practising Psycho-Analysis

There is a simple way to prevent that without blocking parents who are already inside the baby sitter's trusted fold. If the values in `eventStart` and `eventEnd` are encrypted, they must be encrypted with a value available to all trusted parents. If the evil parents know Chris's `idHash` value, they can also figure out p_m.

Section 10.2.1 offers an example that extends the baby sitter database with digital signatures.

There are two solutions to this problem. The easiest fix adds a digital signature to each entry, using some public-key algorithm. That is covered in Chapter 10. Another solution is to duplicate every entry, as done in Section 5.2. Every parent gets a unique value of p_m and maybe even of `idHash`. The evil parents may learn their own value of p_m and `idHash`, but they can't see the entries available to others.

Multiple entries like this may be worth the extra disk space if the schedules call for blocking out some people. Creating different versions of `idHash` for each parent may be inefficient, but it can avoid long, complicated `JOIN` operations.

5.6   Conclusions

Translucent Databases can be used by two or more different people to pass along information. Passing some of the columns through a one-way function prevents eavesdroppers and hackers from learning anything from the database. But structuring these calls in the right way does not prevent the database from doing useful work.

The examples in this chapter illustrate how tables can be linked together to provide the right information to the right people without showing anything to others. The translucent solutions also make design simpler. The basic searching and matching tools of the database can be used to look up events on particular days or times. The programmer does not need to recreate these functions or find a way to make them work through layers of encryption. This information stays in the clear, where the database can do its work.

Good translucent design principles minimize the amount of work that must be done by making it possible to rely on previously insecure but effective tools.

5.6.1 Lessons

- Two people can use a database to share information, synchronize their schedules or pass messages by storing the data linked to $f(x)$. Only the two know x, but no casual observer can determine x from the database.

- x can be secret information, like a password; public information, like a name; or a combination of public and secret information.

- A simple way to link data for different people is to compute $f(ab)$, where a and b are some combinations of names, passwords and other information about two people, a and b.

- Sometimes storing multiple copies is inefficient. Several tables can be used to provide multiple access to different people. The data in one table may be stored under $f(x)$. Another table could help Alice, Bob and Charles find the data by linking $f(x)$ to $f(Alice)$, $f(Bob)$, and $f(Charles)$.

- Hiding one column with a one-way function, while leaving others in the clear makes it possible to use built-in functions from the database software.

- More complex tricks can be played with discrete log-based one-way functions. Chapter 12 describes some of them.

Chapter 6

Evolving Data

All the techniques in this book are designed to hide information behind some translucent shield of one-way functions so only the right people can see what's happening. Locking things away in either a virtual or real sense is one way to protect them. Another is to keep moving them around. This chapter describes how to add evolution and change to the database. A quickly shifting and morphing environment is a greater challenge for an attacker.

The solution is simple, at least in the abstract. Instead of using a basic one-way function applied to the data, $h(x)$, use a more complex function that also depends upon time: $h(x, t)$. If the value of $h(x, t)$ shifts over time, then the attacker must not only find a way through the defenses, but must also find a way to time the attack precisely.

The trick is to add time to the mix without disturbing the other translucent qualities of the database. Consider the basic password database containing pairs of user names and the result of sending their passwords through a one-way function: $(name, h(password))$. There are four approaches to adding time to this equation:

Counters Add a counter to the mix sent to the one-way function: $h(counter,-password)$. The value of the counter starts at 1 and increases each time a new password is used. That approach calls for both sides to know the *password* so the value can be computed.

Clocks Add the actual time to the one-way function computations: $h(\text{"2002}-04-01\ 12:45\text{"}, password)$. A person presenting a value should verify it is computed with the correct time. If synchronization is a problem, the precision can be reduced by rounding off the time stamps and/or allowing adjacent ones like $h(\text{"2002}-04-01\ 12:44\text{"}, password)$ and $h(\text{"2002}-04-01\ 12:46\text{"}, password)$.

Chains Let $h^2(x) = h(h(x))$, $h^3(x) = h(h(h(x)))$ and so on. The sequence of values, $\{h^n(x), h^{n-1}(x), \ldots, h(x), x\}$, forms a chain of one-way answers that are easy to compute if you know x. You simply begin with x and work backwards. But computing the chain in the other direction is presumed to be practically impossible when you begin with $h^n(x)$. This means that the chain of values can act like an evolving password. The first time, use the value $h^n(x)$ as the access code. The second time, use $h^{n-1}(x)$ and so on.

The person checking the chain of passwords does not need to know x itself. Each new value can be compared to the previous value. If someone offers $h^i(x)$, then this can be compared to $h^{i+1}(x)$ by computing $h(h^i(x))$. That means someone can begin the process by offering $h^n(x)$. At each step, the person can offer a new version from the chain.

The best choice for h is usually a traditional cryptographically secure hash function. In these cases, the technique is often called a *hash chain*.

Hybrids Any of these three can be combined in a hybrid. In the most extreme case, a system might use $h^i(counter, timestamp, x)$. Counters can easily be combined with chains. Let $h^2(x) = h(2, h(1, x))$, $h^3(x) = h(3, h(2, h(1, x)))$ etc.

Combining time stamps is a bit more complicated. The time can't be mixed into the chain when the values of $h^n(x)$ are first computed. If there's no fixed schedule for using the values, then there's no way to know when the individual values will be presented. The best solution is to round off the time stamps and create a new chain for each time unit, like the day or week.

All these techniques are useful tools, but some are more translucent than others. That is, some resist attack better than others.

The first two solutions, the counter- and clock-based functions, call for both sides of a transaction to know the value of x, often the password. That may be acceptable when two parties are exchanging data, but it is less acceptable in a computer database. Using either solution requires storing the password in the clear, where it might be compromised.

The chain of one-way-function answers does not call for keeping x around. The database can store $h^{i+1}(x)$ while awaiting $h^i(x)$. Only someone who knows the entire chain can generate this value.

There are many ways to use changing data like this, but the obvious solution is in a password database. The first time, the person presents $h^n(pass-word)$, the second time the person presents $h^{n-1}(password)$, etc. After each visit, the value in the password database is updated with the latest value. Only someone who knows the right value in the chain can add more.

That has some advantages over the traditional solution. Anyone who eavesdrops on the connection between the user and the database can't reuse the information. The password changes each time.

6.1   An Auction Example

Here's an example of using evolving data in an auction system. Each person uses a chain of MD5 hash values to place and increase bids. The database uses the values as the identification and allows people to update their bids only if they present the next (or maybe we should say previous) value in the chain.

The database of bids is created by an SQL command:

```
CREATE TABLE bidTable (auctionId INTEGER, id CHAR(32),
counter INTEGER, bid INTEGER);
```

The auctionId contains the number of the lot, and bid contains the value of the bid in pennies. The id is the typical 32 characters containing a hexadecimal representation of an MD5 result. It could probably be stored as raw bytes with better results, but it would be harder to debug. The counter field keeps track of which element in the hash chain was presented as an identification. It starts at 100 in this example and counts down. This is mainly used as a fail-safe mechanism to help users with forgotten passwords.

Here's some of the sample Java code using JDBC drivers to start the communications with the database and create some PreparedStatement objects. The code would probably be called by a servlet or maybe some other gateway to the auction system.

```
public void init(){
 MD5Bean=new MD5();
 dw=new DatabaseWrapper();
 dw.init();
 initPreparedStatements();
}

PreparedStatement searchBids,addNewBid, maxBid;

public void initPreparedStatements(){
 String q="SELECT bid,counter FROM bidTable  ";
 q=q+"WHERE id=? AND auctionId=? ;";
 searchBids=dw.createPreparedStatement(q);
 q="INSERT INTO bidTable SET ";
 q=q+"id=?,auctionId=?,bid=?,counter=? ;";
 addNewBid=dw.createPreparedStatement(q);
 q="SELECT max(bid) FROM bidTable WHERE auctionId=?;";
 maxBid=dw.createPreparedStatement(q);
}
```

The JDBC code is hidden in the DatabaseWrapper Bean. The searchBids query will lookup up bids using the ID to ensure that the chain to the first bid is correct. The addNewBid fucntiondoes exactly that. The maximum bid on the current auction comes from executing maxBid.

6.1.1   The First Bid

The first bid for a person would probably include some greater preparations. An auction house might check your credit history or see whether you've been a reputable bidder before. When that is finished, it would recognize your bid with this code:

```
public boolean acceptFirstBid(int auctionId,
                String id,
                int amount){
 try{
  maxBid.setInt(1,auctionId);
  ResultSet max=maxBid.executeQuery();
  max.next();
  int maximum=max.getInt(1);
  if (amount<maximum){
     System.out.println("Under bid:"+id+" amount:"+amount);
  } else {
     addNewBid.setInt(2,auctionId);
     addNewBid.setString(1,id);
     addNewBid.setInt(3,amount);
     addNewBid.setInt(4,counterStart);
     addNewBid.executeUpdate();
     return true;
  }
 } catch (SQLException e){
  System.out.println("SQL Exception:"+e);
 }
 return false;
}
```

The method `acceptFirstBid` first uses the `maxBid PreparedStatement` to ensure that the bid is worth making. If it is, then it inserts the bid using the `addNewBid PreparedStatement`. The `counterStart` is set equal to 100 for now.

6.1.2   Adding New Bids

Once the first bid is accepted, later bids can be added to the database quickly. There is no need to run a credit check or examine a password database each time. If the value of $h(h^i(x)) = h^{i+1}(x)$, then the bidder has provided the next/previous value in the MD5 chain.

More complex versions might include digital signatures described in Chapter 10 that guarantee the bid.

This code uses this method as $h(x)$:

```
public String nextValue(String x){
  MD5Bean.clear();
  MD5Bean.Update(x);
  return MD5Bean.asHex();
}
```

Adding a new bid is simple. The function `updateBid` uses these steps:

1. Checks the maximum bid on the table to make sure that this new bid is valid.

2. Takes `id`, the new item in the chain, and computes `nextValue(id)`.

3. Searches the table for that value. It should appear only once.

4. Grabs the counter and decreases it by one.

5. Adds the new bid, using the `addNewBid PreparedStatement`.

The following code doesn't need to access the password database or any ancillary databases. It operates only upon the `bidTable` table. There is no need to encrypt any of the extra information about the value of the bid to provide security.

```
public boolean updateBid(int auctionId, String id, int amount){
  try{

    maxBid.setInt(1,auctionId);
    ResultSet max=maxBid.executeQuery();
    max.next();
    int maximum=max.getInt(1);
    if (amount<=maximum){
      System.out.println("Under bid:"+id+" amount:"+amount);
    } else {
      String oldValue=nextValue(id);
      //now get last bid
      searchBids.setString(1,oldValue);
      searchBids.setInt(2,auctionId);
      ResultSet rs=searchBids.executeQuery();
      if (rs.next()){
        int bid=rs.getInt("bid");// or 1
        int counter=rs.getInt("counter"); // or 2
        // test answer and update the database.
        counter--;
        addNewBid.setInt(2,auctionId);
        addNewBid.setString(1,id);
        addNewBid.setInt(3,amount);
        addNewBid.setInt(4,counter);
        addNewBid.executeUpdate();
        return true;
      } else {
        System.out.print("Unfound bid:"+id);
        System.out.println(" on auction:"+auctionId);
      }
    }
  } catch (SQLException e){
    System.out.println("SQL Exception:"+e);
  }
  return false;
}
```

6.1.3 Creating Bids

The client's software must create the MD5 chains and maybe store them. This example assumes that recalculating the entire chain each time is simpler than storing the last value sent in. The `makeBid` takes a person's password and hashes it one time to create $h(password)$. Then it hashes this again `count` times. The initial value of `count` for creating a new bid in this example is 100.

```
public void makeBid(int auctionId,
                                    String password,
                                    int count,int amount){
  String id=nextValue(password); // this is h(x).
  for (int i=0;i<count;i++){
    id=nextValue(id);
  }
// send the information through a network connection.
//where it is processed like this:
  updateBid(auctionId,id, amount);
}
```

Recreating the entire hash chain in this example makes sense if count is a reasonable value. Stored information can be compromised. Presumably the value of password is easy to remember, but $h^i(password)$ will always be a 32-character hexadecimal number.

Here's an example of a bidding war between two people:

auctionId	id	counter	bid
1001	6db41045b4afa5823f51fdd7e80d0fd0	100	100
1001	25544ab0002e55327afd2213170b98f3	100	102
1001	bdf8c87bbb9f02fd840d68a5fcc92e6a	99	103
1001	49b1c7387aa0dee16282d0abca76b8b1	99	104
1001	b578ad0e771cd0f57172bbf75fa17674	98	110
1001	0dd40869fb8b29ba42cd20ab49ca4455	98	115

The first person used the password "swordfish", and the second used "no password".

6.1.4   The Value of the Counter Function

This value held in the counter serves little purpose in this version. If the bidder's computer will recompute the hash chains at each step, the bidder's computer must remember the value. If anything, the counter leaks information. It is easy to look at the table of bids and figure out a lot about who's participating and who isn't from the counter value alone. That can also be recovered by hashing the values in id and linking them together into a chain.

The counter's main value is helping the bidder's computer recover from losing track of the right value. In practice, it might be stored in a different table bound to the person's real identity. If someone's software crashed and the user lost the value of counter, the person's computer could ask this table for the right value. In this example, it was rolled into this one table for the purpose of illustration.

The example in the code above offers a fair amount of anonymity. There is no personal information in bidTable. An auction house could forget the identity of the the person who was bidding after it authorized the first bid.

The winner could demand the goods by providing the next/previous value in the hash chain. Only the rightful bidder's computer would know that value.

6.1.5   Better Hash Functions

A better implementation of the function could use a slightly more sophisticated version of $h(x)$:

```
public String nextValue(String x, int auctionId){
  MD5Bean.clear();
  MD5Bean.Update(x+auctionId);  return
  MD5Bean.asHex();
}
```

Mixing in the value of `auctionId` allows the bidder to use the same password with different auctions. The hash chains will be different, although it's not clear if that is essential. If $h^i(x) = h(h(\ldots h(h(x + auctionId))\ldots))$, then the chains will still be different. The `auctionId` needs to be added only in at the beginning.

Another approach chooses a random value of the password x for each chain. That value, of course, must be stored securely because it can't be remembered like a password.

It doesn't seem likely that mixing the real time into the computation of h would help this application.

6.2   Working With Encryption

The evolving identification codes can also be used to scramble the information at each step for some extra security. If you're going to encrypt some entries in some of the fields, then you may want to re-encrypt them with each visit.

Here's one solution. Let $f_k(data)$ be an encryption function protecting the *data* using the key k, and $h^i(x)$ is ith element of the chain.

The database holds the information encrypted with f using $k = h^i(x)$. Every time someone wants to use the data, the database follows these steps:

1. The database gets a copy of $h^{i-1}(x)$.

2. The database computes $h(h^{i-1}(x))$ and uses this to decrypt *data*.

3. The database does its work.

4. The database re-encrypts *data* using $k = h^{i-1}(x)$.

5. The database forgets $h^{i-1}(x)$.

The information in the database is still vulnerable when it is unencrypted, but the rest of the time it is protected by a shifting key. Each key presented must be different, and an eavesdropper can't reuse a previous value to get at the information.

This solution isn't completely secure, though, because an eavesdropper with root access to the database can use the last value sent along the line, $h^{i-1}(x)$, to compute f. The value can't be presented to the shell software doing the work, but it can be combined with access to the data itself.

This solution has some advantages. The client does not need to remember an endlessly changing string of passwords. It can compute $h^i(x)$ from i and x. In fact, the value of i can be stored in the database for extra flexibility.

6.3 Conclusions

Changing the information in the database with time increases the security of the system. Past attacks won't work in the future because the information keeps shifting underneath.

The one-way functions in this chapter are almost always used with fast hash functions like MD5 or SHA. Recomputing the chain is often too cumbersome with exponential arithmetic.

Public-key functions with trapdoors have some advantages. Using them effectively creates three different values that can be distributed to provide control: the public key, the private key and the value of x at the beginning of the chain. Anyone with the public key can check one step in the chain. Anyone with the public key and x can recompute the entire chain. Anyone with just the private key can recompute the entire chain. These three values can be redistributed in funny ways. The public key might not be truly public. It might be given to only one person. The private key would act like the root password. There are many choices. It's not clear who would have an application that might need this type of control, but it would be interesting to watch it work.

6.3.1 Lessons

- The chain of values $\{h^n(x), h^{n-1}(x), \ldots, h^2(x), h(x), x\}$ can serve as a list of access codes that is easy to store and recompute.

- Anyone with $h^i(x)$ can easily test the validity of $h^{i-1}(x)$ with one computation of h, but no one should be able to compute this value without knowing x.

- Other one-way functions like exponentiation modulo a prime work well, but they're less efficient than cryptographically secure hash functions.

- Changing the access code with each new event prevents eavesdroppers from abusing the database. Each event needs a new key that can't be guessed from the information in the database.

Chapter 7

Sharing

There are times when a single database can't be trusted, even if the data is massaged by all the possible encryption algorithms and one-way functions. In most cases, the problem is more political than mathematical because the real issue is more one of control than security. Putting all of the information in one location makes it possible for whoever controls that database to have control of how and when it is used.

Cryptographic researchers have an answer for this problem, too. Algorithms for sharing a secret make it possible for several people or their databases to control the release of information. The algorithms offer a surprising amount of flexibility, making it possible to keep the information locked away until some subset of k people out of a group of n agree to open it up.

Splitting the information up into separate databases can solve several tricky political problems by making several databases equal partners for controlling the information. If two companies work together on a joint product, they may battle over who gets the customer lists. Putting them into two split databases ensures that each company can lock out the other if there is a dispute. The potential threat of mutual assured destruction often helps keep relationships in good condition.

Sometimes, control of a crucial asset may require two or more groups to agree. Firing nuclear missiles, for instance, needs two soldiers (or sailors) to pull the trigger. Splitting the data into two databases gives two system administrators and two corporate bureaucracies power over the data. That may be twice the inertia, but it may also give twice the resistance to abuse.

Some of the basic algorithms in Chapter 13 also trust multiple databases and let people retrieve information without exposing what they want to get.

7.1   The Algorithms

There are several different algorithms for splitting information into separate pieces, and most of them are mathematically equivalent to embedding the secret value in a line or plane through some space and then distributing points on the line or plane. Once enough points are available, the line or plane can be reconstructed and the secret value rediscovered.

Here's a simple example of splitting a number c in a way that requires two people to work together to rediscover c:

1. Choose a random value of m and let $f(x) = mx + c$. This line goes through the y axis ($x = 0$) at the point $(0, c)$.

2. Choose n different values at random: $\{x_1, x_2, \ldots, x_n\}$. Make sure that $x_i \neq 0, \forall i$.

3. Give n people a pair $(x_i, f(x_i))$.

Any two of the n people can get together and use their points to determine the slope m and where the line goes through the y axis, c. Each person alone, though, can't infer that information.

If you need to force more than two people to agree, then use a plane in a greater dimensional space. If you need k people to agree, use a k-dimensional hyperplane. You can still distribute n points on the plane.

7.1.1   More Precise Algorithms

The easiest way to understand secret sharing is to imagine lines in infinite space, but that may not be the best way to use the algorithms. Computers usually do a good job representing infinite imaginary surfaces, but errors can creep into calculations when the numbers get too big. Round off errors and overflow mistakes can foul the arithmetic.

A better solution is to use the same mathematics in a more restricted space. Doing the calculations with integers modulo a prime number is one solution that is often compatible with other one-way functions.

A faster solution is to use a different conception of numbers. Adi Shamir used k bit vectors or $(k-1)^{th}$-order polynomials with coefficients of either 0 or 1.[Sha79] The XOR function is equivalent to addition for bit vectors while the AND function is equivalent to multiplication. All of the standard rules for algebra apply and work. The results can be a bit confusing if you're not used to working with anything but regular integers, but the math does follow.

Here's a basic algorithm for distributing a secret, c, between n people:

1. Choose $n - 1$ random values with the same number of bits as c. Call these $\{x_1, x_2, \ldots, x_{n-1}\}$.

2. Now choose x_n so that all the values, x_i, add up to n. Let $\oplus$ stand for the exclusive OR operation. ($0 \oplus 0 = 0, 0 \oplus 1 = 1, 1 \oplus 0 = 1, 1 \oplus 1 = 0$.) That is the equivalent of addition in this domain. Let $x_n = c \oplus x_1 \oplus x_2 \oplus \ldots \oplus x_{n-1}$.

3. Distribute the values of $\{x_1 \ldots, x_n\}$ to n different people.

The entire group of n people must join together to reassemble their values and find c. Any subset will yield only random values. All are completely random except one value. The last is just a function of all the random ones and the secret value being split up.

Using random numbers with the same number of bits as c guarantees that each bit of each x_i is just as likely to be a 0 or a 1. Doing arithmetic modulo p does not produce this result because there are no primes of the form 2^i, although it is possible to find values that are close. The exclusive OR operation is built into most CPUs and executes in one clock cycle.

This approach can also be extended to allow any subset of k people out of the n to assemble c, but it is beyond the range of this book.

7.1.2 More Efficient Algorithms

In most cases, the best way to share access to a large file is to encrypt it with a key and then split the key up amoung the groups, using a standard algorithm. Another solution is to encrypt the file twice and distribute parts of the file itself. Only someone who recovers all parts can decrypt the file.

That approach calls for an encryption algorithm that propagates changes in the data throughout the file. Several standard algorithms encrypt data in k-bit blocks and arrange for the results of one block to affect the next block. This is often called *autokeying* or *cipher block chaining*. There are many different approaches with different advantages.

Here's one solution. Let the file consist of blocks $B_1, B_2, \ldots$. Let $f_{k_i}(B_i)$ be the result of encrypting block B_i with the key k_i. The result of encrypting one block can be chained together with the next by XORing in the result with the key, $k_i = k \oplus f_{k_{i-1}}(B_{i-i}), \forall k \geq 2$. Let k be the key for the entire file, and $k_1 = k$.

If that algorithm is used once, a change in block B_i will affect every block after it but not the blocks that come before it. If this encryption process is repeated twice for the file, then every block will depend upon every other one. On the second pass, replace k with $k \oplus f_{k_n}(B_n)$. All parts must be present to decrypt the file.

This solution works only with long files. Each piece should be long enough to prevent brute-force attacks designed to try all possible values. If a file has 64 bits, it would not make sense to split it into eight pieces because there are only $2^8(256)$ possible values for any one piece.

7.1.3 Adding Sophistication

The basic algorithm for splitting a secret is useful, but it has one basic weakness. Whoever recovers the n parts and reconstructs the secret can now use the secret again and again and again. The information can't be resplit or put back in a bottle.

Similar solution uses the intractability of the discrete-log problem to cloak the actions. Here's a way to use a public-key algorithm to split control of the key between n people. Anyone can encrypt a message, but all n people must agree to decrypt it. If they do decrypt one message, the results still can't be used to decrypt the next message sent to the group.

The algorithm uses n private keys or secret values: $\{x_1, x_2, \ldots, x_n\}$. The public key is $g^{x_1} g^{x_2} \ldots g^{x_n} \bmod p$ where p is a prime number and g is a generator.

These steps send a message to the group:

1. The sender chooses a random value y and raises the public key, $g^{x_1} g^{x_2} \ldots g^{x_n} \bmod p$, to the yth power. That is, computes $(g^{x_1} g^{x_2} \ldots g^{x_n} \bmod p)^y \bmod p$.

2. Encrypt the message using this value as the key.

3. Compute $g^y \bmod p$.

4. Send both the encrypted message and $g^y \bmod p$. Discard y.

When the message arrives, the group can decrypt it with these steps:

1. Each member is given $g^y \bmod p$.

2. Each member computes $(g^y \bmod p)^{x_i} \bmod p = g^{x_i y} \bmod p$ where x_i is each person's private key.

3. All the members pool their values and multiply them together modulo p.

4. This value $g^{y(x_1 + x_2 + \ldots + x_n)} \bmod p$ is the same one used by the sender. Use it as the key to decrypt the message.

This algorithm produces a different value every time it is used. Decrypting one message does not reveal the secret keys to everyone, nor does it provide any information that can be used to decrypt the next message.

7.2   Nuclear Launch Codes

The correct codes for launching nuclear missiles are such valuable commodities that they make an ideal example for splitting information between databases. No one person controls the database, so no one person can launch the missiles. Each can audit requests and authenticate them in a variety of ways to confirm that they're correct.

This example splits the codes into four parts and distributes them among four tables: base0, base1, base2 and base3. The nomenclature was chosen to make automating the process easier.

Here are the commands that created the databases:

```
CREATE TABLE base0 (missile CHAR(32), code BIGINT);
```

```
CREATE TABLE base1 (missile CHAR(32), code BIGINT);

CREATE TABLE base2 (missile CHAR(32), code BIGINT);

CREATE TABLE base3 (missile CHAR(32), code BIGINT);
```

The name of each missile is stored in the clear in a 32-character array.

The Java code for accessing the databases uses a number of Prepared-Statements created when the class file is begun. The launch codes are split into n parts specified by the value of the constant shares. Here's the initialization code:

```
DatabaseWrapper dw=new DatabaseWrapper();
java.util.Random ran;

public void init(){
 dw.init();
 ran=new java.util.Random();
  initPS();
}

final int shares=4;

PreparedStatement[][] ps;

public void initPS(){
  ps=new PreparedStatement[shares][2];
  String q;
  for (int i=0;i<shares;i++){
  q="INSERT INTO base"+i+" SET missile=?, code=?;";
  ps[i][0]=dw.createPreparedStatement(q);
  q="SELECT code FROM base"+i+" WHERE missile=?;";
  ps[i][1]=dw.createPreparedStatement(q);
 }
}
```

7.2.1 Adding Launch Codes

The launch codes are split into shares parts by setting all but one to be a random number, and then setting the last to be the XOR of the rest and the code.

```
public long[] splitLong(long c,
                                      int number){
 long[] ans=new long[number];
 long x=0;
 long t;
 for (int i=1;i<number;i++){
  t=ran.nextLong();
  x=x^t;
  ans[i]=t;
 }
 ans[0]=c^x;
 return ans;
```

```
}

public void splitCode(String missile, long c){
  try{
    long[] values=splitLong(c,shares);
    for (int i=0;i<shares;i++){
      ps[i][0].setString(1,missile);
      ps[i][0].setLong(2,values[i]);
      ps[i][0].executeUpdate();
    }

  } catch (Exception e){
    System.out.println("Problems adding missile code:"+e);
  }
}
```

Here are four tables showing the result of adding three missiles:

missile	code
KFX-4244	5887186030757112284
KFX-8333	3890514967659699042
KFX-1452	-2205185510378140486

missile	code
KFX-4244	8703618182130622361
KFX-8333	-1667008005169276721
KFX-1452	305500755453386641

missile	code
KFX-4244	-3492968287992323254
KFX-8333	-2503766294981816324
KFX-1452	-5872506014442219819

missile	code
KFX-4244	-1802440653164416805
KFX-8333	272130362909429488
KFX-1452	5465235535485538706

7.2.2   Recovering the Code

Finding the launch code is as simple as querying all the databases and XORing together the result.

```
public long recoverCode(String missile){
  long ans=0;
  ResultSet rs;
```

```
try{
  for (int i=0;i<shares;i++){
    ps[i][1].setString(1,missile);
    rs=ps[i][1].executeQuery();
    if (rs.next()){
      ans=ans^rs.getLong(1);
    } else {
      System.out.println("Trouble recovering from database "+i);
    }
  }

} catch (Exception e){
  System.out.println("Problems recovering missile code:"+e);
}
System.out.println("Missile "+missile+" has code:"+ans);
return ans;
}
```

7.2.3 Adding More Security

This solution splits the responsibility for the launch codes among four databases. The rules for access to each of the databases are left out of the examples, but they are presumably strict enough to prevent someone from gaining access to more than one database. A hacker or curious system administrator can't do anything with the information in the databases without gaining access to all of them.

This solution is probably sufficient, but there's no reason why another one-way layer can't be put in the person's way. One simple barrier hashes the missile's name with a password and the name of the database. Each entry for the missile is different, so there is no way to correlate the tables.

If someone does manage to grab all four databases, there's no way to tell which missile matches which part unless you know both the password and the names of the missile.

Here's the code:

```
public String constructMissileName(String missile,
 String password,
 String database){
 MD5Bean.clear();
 MD5Bean.Update(password);
 MD5Bean.Update(missile);
 MD5Bean.Update(database);
 return MD5Bean.asHex();
}


public void splitCode(String missile, long c){
 String nm;
 try{
   long[] values=splitLong(c,shares);
   for (int i=0;i<shares;i++){
     nm=constructMissileName(missile,"swordfish","base"+i);
```

```
      ps[i][0].setString(1,nm);
      ps[i][0].setLong(2,values[i]);
      ps[i][0].executeUpdate();
  }

} catch (Exception e){
  System.out.println("Problems adding missile code:"+e);
}
}
```

Here's the result after adding three missiles to the databases:

missile — code
88051b5471392775e99e063a80c09b45 — -119835343787049117
6c769c1dc01fffea97341e4c6d2c712a — 1761517375766510678
9c47d03ac412c9a3f9897ea14e7fa537 — -1948886059326911251

missile — code
63d934b85077ff116d0d3bd9bab0f46e — 8891232736897281699
f8c9e3ef97dde3cc6a298a03e04e3a43 — -2346903544962495451
e45e7467bb364ff40f570578101a62be — -967665374181373816

missile — code
ac490eb5561a28f1a179c7fe2546ed8d — -5946670664101867496
e7d24304807641e3c6a7ac09b5a51a2a — 485239692895635747
b24a24aa0aa0047b78db651c30ea1c90 — -1472608860763344988

missile — code
8201c79ace0ee7da1788d39c8b47b6f1 — 2903535311376114700
4fcf75dcb9a162062553402ed5aa537c — -4492375815335764723
d28a1794d8a72d993d2ac484e3f1d736 — -146862835796492371

Of course, any one-way function might be used if a backdoor is needed. Using a different password for each database might make sense.

7.3 A Public-Key Example

The public-key algorithms described above in Section 7.1.3 are excellent tools for building databases in environments with little mutual trust. If several people must approve opening a record, then these equations make it possible for all of them to sign off on every database transaction.

A good example of this is a suggestion Box, a seemingly benign tool that can often create dissent. While many suggestion boxes are filled with happy ideas about saving money, some are viewed as tools for political intrigue. In the most extreme cases, the suggestion boxes are mechanisms for anonymously reporting crime.

In sensitive realms, it may make sense to have a committee open the messages in the suggestion box. If a single employee opened the messages, any that the employee didn't like could be destroyed.

This code is very similar to the message-passing example described in Section 4.2.2. In that case, a message was sent to one person encrypted by a public key. Only the holder of the corresponding private key could decrypt it. This database also stores messages sent to a group encrypted with the group's public key, but this database requires the entire group to work together to decrypt it.

There are few real differences because the math is so similar. The biggest difference is that this code can decode particular messages. Each row in the `messages2` table comes with a `mac`, a message authentication code computed from the message itself. It acts like a surrogate for the message itself so all the people in the process can have a unique name for the message. The odds of creating an identical value of `mac` with a different message are quite low. Here's the SQL line for creating the table:

```
CREATE TABLE messages2 (toName TINYTEXT, fromName TINYTEXT,
m BLOB, geey TINYTEXT, mac CHAR(32));
```

The example uses the same `pubkeys` table from Section 4.2.2.

Section 8.4 uses similar mathematics to build an identification card for a user who doesn't always want to expose all their personal information. A person can show his or her age and weight, but not his or her height and Social Security number.

7.3.1 Adding a Message

A person sending a message to one person or the group doesn't know whether the recipient is a single person or a group. The database `pubkeys` is just a table mapping `name` to values of g, $g^x \bmod p$ and p. The value of x may be held by one person or a group. The sender calculates a random value of y, encrypts the message with a value derived from $(g^x \bmod p)^y \bmod p$, and bundles it together with $g^y \bmod p$. The value of `mac` comes from hashing the entire message.

This example continues to use the built-in `ENCODE` function in `MySQL` to encrypt the data.

Note that these examples use MySQL's `ENCODE` *function for illustration. Better encryption functions are available.*

```
public void insertMessage(String from,
                          String to,
                          String message){
  String findQuery="SELECT * FROM pubkeys WHERE name='";
  findQuery=findQuery+to+"';";

  MD5Bean.clear();
  MD5Bean.Update(message);
  String mac=MD5Bean.asHex();

  try{
    ResultSet rs=dw.executeQuery(findQuery);
    rs.next(); // get the first match.

    String gee=rs.getString("gee");
    String pea=rs.getString("pea");
    String geex=rs.getString("geex");

    BigInteger gx=new BigInteger(geex);
```

```
BigInteger p=new BigInteger(pea);
BigInteger y=new BigInteger(760,5,new Random());
BigInteger g=new BigInteger(gee);
BigInteger gy=g.modPow(y,p);

// Compute secret key.
BigInteger key=gx.modPow(y,p);
MD5Bean.clear();
MD5Bean.Update(key.toByteArray());

// Construct query.
StringBuffer query=new StringBuffer();
query.append("INSERT INTO messages2 VALUES('");
query.append(to);
query.append("','");
query.append(from);
query.append("',ENCODE('");
query.append(message);
query.append("','");
query.append(MD5Bean.asHex());
query.append("'),'");
query.append(gy.toString());
query.append("','");
query.append(mac);
query.append("');");

dw.executeQuery(query.toString());
System.out.println(query);
} catch (java.sql.SQLException e){

}

}
```

7.3.2 Retrieving the Message

The group shares access to the messages2 table, but the members can't read the messages in it without everyone working together. This example shows two functions. The first, recoverOneKey, is used by an individual person to take $g^y \bmod p$ and return $(g^y \bmod p)^{x_i} \bmod p$, where x_i is the person's secret key. The second, aggregateAndDecode, combines all the keys to find the key to decode the message.

Here is how the functions may be used:

1. Someone decides to read a particular message with mac.

2. The person sends a message asking group members to compute the BigInteger corresponding to $(g^y \bmod p)^{x_i} \bmod p$ for that value of mac.

3. Everyone uses recoverOneKey and forwards the result to a central actor.

4. Everyone is given the array of BigIntegers.

5. Everyone decodes the message using aggregateAndDecode.

```
Public BigInteger recoverOneKey(String nm,
                                String passphrase,
                                String messageMac){
  MD5Bean.clear();
  MD5Bean.Update("Translucent Databases rock.");
  MD5Bean.Update(passphrase);
  byte[] hashedPass=MD5Bean.Final();
  BigInteger x=new BigInteger(hashedPass);

  String findQuery="SELECT * FROM messages2 WHERE mac='";
  findQuery=findQuery+messageMac+"';";

  String findPeaQuery="SELECT * FROM pubkeys WHERE name='";
  findPeaQuery=findPeaQuery+nm+"';";

  try{
    // find the prime number.
    ResultSet rsp=dw.executeQuery(findPeaQuery);
    rsp.next();// the first public key.
    String pea=rsp.getString("pea");
    BigInteger p=new BigInteger(pea);


    ResultSet rs=dw.executeQuery(findQuery);
    rs.next(); // get the first match.

    // compute key
    String geey=rs.getString("geey");
    BigInteger gy=new BigInteger(geey);
  BigInteger key=gy.modPow(x,p);
    return key;
  } catch (java.sql.SQLException e){

  }
  return null;

}


public void aggregateAndDecode(BigInteger[] parts,
                               String messageMac){
 try{
    int len=parts.length;
    BigInteger ans=BigInteger.valueOf(1);
    for (int i=0;i<len;i++){
       ans=ans.multiply(parts[i]);
    }
    MD5Bean.clear();
    MD5Bean.Update(ans.toByteArray());

    // Blob b=rs.getBlob("m");
    // use this to decode the data locally.
    // or
    String query="SELECT DECODE(m,'"+ MD5Bean.asHex();
    query=query+"') FROM messages2 WHERE mac='"+messageMac+"';";
    ResultSet rs2=dw.executeQuery(query);
    rs2.next();// get the first row only here.
```

```
    System.out.println(rs2.getString(1));

 } catch (java.sql.SQLException e){

  }

}
```

These tools offer a bit more secrecy than the previous example. Once a message is decrypted, it stays decrypted. But the private keys of each individual remain secret. New messages can't be decoded until everyone agrees.

7.4   Conclusions

Splitting information between databases provides control to everyone who owns one of the databases. Everyone must agree before the data is taken apart. It is an effective way to separate and share power.

7.4.1   Lessons

- A file can be shared between n people by encrypting it and breaking up the key into n parts.

- The security of that depends upon the size of the part given to each person.

- The simplest solution can be weak. If there are m bits in the key, then giving $\frac{m}{n}$ bits to each person may not provide enough complexity if m is small. The Advanced Encryption Standard (AES), for instance, uses 80-bit keys in its simplest form. Splitting one between 10 people means each person gets 8 bits. If $n - 1$ people get together, then they need to try $2^8(256)$ possible combinations to recover the last person's key.

- The best way to break up a secret, c, into n parts is to create $n-1$ random numbers, $x_1, x_2, \ldots, x_{n-1}$, then set $x_n = c \oplus x_1 \oplus x_2 \oplus \ldots \oplus x_{n-1}$. This means that $c = x_1 \oplus x_2 \oplus \ldots \oplus x_n$. If c has m bits, then each part also has m bits, and it's impossible to guess one person's value.

- More complex algorithms can split up a secret so that any subset of k people from the group of n can reconstruct the secret value. These can be quite practical if any of the people holding the information may be detained, killed or prevented from reconstructing the secret value.

- Encrypting a large file twice and then splitting the file into pieces is another way to split a secret.

- Using public-key functions can provide reusable secrets. Pulling them together once does not destroy them. The system can offer a long-term working mechanism for sharing information.

Chapter 8

Revelation

There will be times it makes sense for someone to strip away the translucent barriers and unveil the information in the database. That person may want to take credit for an anonymous story, reveal some medical records to a doctor, or perhaps unveil their predications for the Superbowl winner. There's no reason why the data in a translucent database must remain secret forever.

Cryptographers generally refer to that process as *bit commitment,* a reference to the time when the idea was first used to force someone to lock in a choice of one bit without showing it. The algorithms let someone choose heads or tails, 0 or 1, or left or right without revealing that to the other party. When everything is over, the value can be shown in such a way that no cheating can happen. The person who chose heads cannot quickly juggle the values to make it look as if the choice was tails.

The basic algorithm looks like this:

1. A person decides to commit to bit b.

2. The person choose two random strings, r_1 and r_2.

3. The person computes $h(r_1 r_2 b)$ and publishes that value along with r_1. Both b and r_2 remain a secret.

4. Everyone who wants to test the outcome saves those two values.

5. Time passes by. The coin is flipped or the game is played, and the winner is decided.

6. The person shows b and r_2.

7. Everyone checks to see whether the newly revealed b and r_2 combine with r_1 to produce the same value of $h(r_1 r_2 b)$. If they do, the person's prediction holds. There was no cheating.

Bit commitment is a simple way to lock information into a sealed envelope. The results don't need to be limited to a single bit. The value of b could be any string. As b becomes longer and more unpredictable, the need for r_2 disappears. The main reason we have r_2 is to prevent someone from precomputing $h(r_1 b)$ for all possible values of b. If the size of the set of all possible values is small, then everyone could figure out the predictions ahead of time.

The value of r_1 is also important when b is small. If there were no r_1 in the equation, then a person could search frantically for two strings, r_2 and r'_2, so that $h(r_2 0) = h(r'_2 1)$. If the person wants to show $b = 0$, the person would also reveal r_2. If person wants to reveal $b = 1$, the person would show r'_2, too.

As the value of b becmes longer, more unpredictable and subject to some arbitrary format, there is less need for the random strings, r_1 and r_2. If b is some large XML object that must conform to a complicated set of formatting rules, the odds of finding another b' that fits the formatting rules and produces $h(r_1, r_2, b) = h(r_1, r'_2, b')$ is exceedingly small. Removing r_2 from the equation gives the potential cheater less flexibility.

For most practical purposes, the use of one-way functions in this book is a form of bit commitment. Many of the implementations use a value of r_1 that is hard-coded into the application. The value of r_2 is usually described as a password or passphrase that controls access. The value of b is the person's name or other private information. Although many of the algorithms treat the one-way function as just a one-way function, there's no doubt that it can be used for a form of bit commitment. Someone can always come along and reveal the hidden name and password to the world, opening the records. Sometimes that is useful.

8.1   A Masquerade

Imagine you throw a masquerade party with impenetrable successful costumes that actually make it impossible to determine the identities of the guests. Some people may want to keep their identities secret. Others may want to reveal their costumes after the fact. But how do you prevent people from taking credit for other people's costumes? Force each person to make an entry in your database *before* the party.

Here's a simple two-column SQL database:

```
CREATE TABLE masquerade (name TINYTEXT, costume CHAR(32));
```

A reveler's name is placed in the clear in `name` while the MD5 hash of the person's disguise is locked away in `costume`.

Here's the Java code for hashing the information and inserting it:

```
MD5 MD5Bean=new MD5();
java.util.Random ran;
DatabaseWrapper dw=newDatabaseWrapper();

public void init(){
  dw.init();
```

```
    ran=new java.util.Random();
    initRS();
}


PreparedStatement insert;

public void initRS(){
 String q="INSERTINTO masquerade SET name=?,";
 q=q+"costume=?;";
 insert=dw.createPreparedStatement(q);
}


public voidinsertName(String name, String costume){
  try{
    insert.setString(1,name);

    MD5Bean.clear();
    MD5Bean.Update("Lifeis a masquerade.");
    MD5Bean.Update(costume);
    insert.setString(2,MD5Bean.asHex());
    insert.executeUpdate();
  } catch(SQLException e){
    System.out.println("SQL Exception:"+e);
  }
}
```

The `MD5Bean` computes the hash of `costume` using the phrase, "Life is a masquerade.", as a randomizing initialization vector for the function. A better solution might have the database server generate a random string for each user.

If Bob comes the morning after the party and wants to claim that he was the one with the elaborate pirate's costume, complete with muskets and free gold coins for everyone, well, you can check it out with this function:

```
public void testName(String name, String costume){
  try{
  String st="SELECT costume FROM masquerade WHERE name='"+name+"';"
  ResultSet rs=dw.executeQuery(st);
  if (rs.next()){
    String c1=rs.getString(1);

    MD5Bean.clear();
    MD5Bean.Update("Life is a masquerade.");
    MD5Bean.Update(costume);
    String c2=MD5Bean.asHex();

    if (c1.equals(c2)){
      System.out.println("The hashes match! ");
      System.out.println(name+" was really a "+costume);
    } else {
      System.out.println("The hashes don't match.");
      System.out.println("Did you misspell something?");
    }
  } else {
```

```
     System.out.println("That name can't be found.");
   }
 } catch (SQLException e){
   System.out.println("SQL Exception:"+e);
 }
}
```

If this code is executed:

```
Masquerade m=new Masquerade();
 m.init();

 m.insertName("Harrison Jones","WWII Veteran");
 m.insertName("Constance Harvey","bear");
 m.insertName("Caliope Jones","fox");
 m.insertName("Helen Nell","Summary Judgment");
```

Then this is what the database looks like:

name	costume
Harrison Jones	77f5d05ea632b6ea29e6587d6480f591
Constance Harvey	99e4bb3036c25a4ae27b29066cc5efa6
Caliope Jones	3ff8dda2242673d6265c3ecf38b046ac
Helen Nell	93b00994ffdd1c38b0d94bdafbb6ec83

Judging the security of this solution is difficult. If you know that one reveler used three lowercase letters to describe her costume and another used four, then it should be easy to use a bit of brute force and run all those short words in the dictionary through MD5. Guessing the costume of Harrison Jones or Helen Nell, on the other hand, should be nearly impossible. In fact, Harrison Jones may have trouble taking credit if he doesn't remember the exact spelling and punctuation he used in the entry.

8.2   Lottery

Public lotteries are popular games, but the high stakes and large scale make them prone to cheating. A person with the right printer and some practice can create duplicate tickets. Winning lottery tickets are often exchanged quietly before being claimed because they are an ideal way to launder cash. Gangsters looking for a way to legitimize the pile of currency in their closets can trade the cash for an anonymous winner's ticket. The gangsters suddenly have a legitimate way to explain how they came across their wealth.

The translucent database in this example avoids all these problems and provides gamblers a bit of privacy and security. The bets are held in a vast database open to all. Anyone can audit the result by downloading a copy before the event. After the numbers are drawn, the winner can come forward and claim the prize. Until that point, no one will know who was playing the game and no one will who had a chance to win. Afterward, everyone scrutinizing the game can be certain that the winner truly made the bet beforehand.

8.2.1 Paying for the Ticket

This example contains two different kinds of commitments. The bettor will commit to a choices of numbers in the next section. In this section, the lottery owner creates "coins" by committing to their value. This commitment bundles a unique serial number for the digital coin with a digital signature that guarantees it. The two values bundled together create a coin.

A bettor must include a special token or coin to pay for the bet. These coins are created and distributed by a special secure server in much the same way that carnivals sell tickets for rides and games. The job of handling the money is centralized in a secure place, and everyone else can just take tickets.

Here's the SQL table for keeping records:

```
CREATE TABLE coins (idNum INT, dateSold TIMESTAMP,
dateRedeemed TIMESTAMP);
```

The idNum is a random integer that acts as the serial number for the coin. It may make sense to use a long integer for this. The fields dateSold and dateRedeemed just keep track of when the coin was created and used.

Here's some simple code for issuing a coin for a particular serial number:

```
public boolean testCoin(int i){
 try{
   String q="SELECT * FROM coins WHERE idNum="+i;
   ResultSet rs=dw.executeQuery(q);
   return rs.next();
 } catch (SQLException e){
   System.out.println("SQL Exception:"+e);
 }
 return false; // failure mode is badly planned here.
}

public String buildCoin(int i){
// code to check that I have not been taken.
 if (testCoin(i)){
   return "Invalid serial number. Choose again.";
 }
 MD5Bean.clear();
 MD5Bean.Update("Serial Num:"+i);
 MD5Bean.Update("It takes a dollar and a dream.");
 String sig=MD5Bean.asHex();
 String qq="INSERT INTO coins VALUES("+i+",NOW(),null);";
 dw.executeUpdate(qq);
 return sig;
}
```

This code is usually run on the secure server issuing the coins, but in the example, there's no extra server for the sake of simplicity. The server takes the serial number and uses `testCoin` to check if it has been used before. The odds of that happening at random are quite low if the serial number is chosen from a large enough set. A lottery company may want to flag people who try to reuse serial numbers as potential fraudsters.

The server creates a signature validating the coin by hashing together the serial number and the phrase "It takes a dollar and a dream." This phrase is the password that guarantees a coin. If it slips out, anyone can counterfeit coins. Using MD5 to create the signatures is faster than using a public-key algorithm, but it makes it impossible to check the signatures without knowing this password phrase.

These coins can be issued well in advance of the time they are used. A person might buy these serial numbers and signature combinations at a local store with a secure terminal. Later, that person can place their bets from any Internet terminal without worrying about security.

8.2.2 Placing Bets

Placing a bet is just the process of computing $h(name, password)$ and $h(name, password, numbers)$. The name and password are sent through a one-way function to preserve a bettor's privacy. The numbers are sent through to preserve the odds of the game. If two people choose the same numbers, they must split the pot if they win. If the `lottery` table is truly public to encourage auditing, then these values must be shielded to prevent people from deliberately avoiding number combinations chosen by others to increase their payoffs. Last-minute bettors get a significant increase in their odds.

Paul Syverson describes a more complex version of this scheme.[Syv98]

Here's the SQL code for creating the database:

```
CREATE TABLE lottery (name CHAR(32), picks CHAR(32), coinNum
INT, coinSig CHAR(32));
```

name holds $h(name, password)$ and picks holds $h(name, password, numbers)$. The `coinNum` is the serial number of a valid coin to pay for the bet. The `coinSig` value should be a valid signature generated by `buildCoin` if the person isn't cheating.

Here's the code for placing a bet:

```
MD5 MD5Bean=new MD5();
java.util.Random ran;
DatabaseWrapper dw=new DatabaseWrapper();

public void init(){
 dw.init();
 ran=new java.util.Random();
 initPS();
}


PreparedStatement insert;
```

```
public void initPS(){
 String q="INSERT INTO lottery SET name=?,";
 q=q+"picks=?,coinNum=?,coinSig=?;";
 insert=dw.createPreparedStatement(q);

}

public void makeBet(String name, String password,
         int p1, int p2, int p3, int p4,
         int p5, int p6){
 int num=ran.nextInt();
 String sig;
 do
   sig=buildCoin(num);
 while (sig.indexOf("Invalid serial")>=0);

 MD5Bean.clear();
 MD5Bean.Update("It takes my dollar and my dream.");
 MD5Bean.Update(name);
 MD5Bean.Update(password);
 String idHash=MD5Bean.asHex();

 MD5Bean.clear();
 MD5Bean.Update("It takes my dollar and my dream.");
 MD5Bean.Update(name);
 MD5Bean.Update(password);

 MD5Bean.Update(""+p1+p2+p3+p4+p5+p6);
 String picks=MD5Bean.asHex();

 try{
   insert.setString(1,idHash);
   insert.setString(2,picks);
   insert.setInt(3,num);
   insert.setString(4,sig);
   insert.executeUpdate();
 } catch (SQLException e){
   System.out.println("SQL Exception:"+e);
 }
}
```

This example includes the initialization code for the class file. The function buildCoin is called from here for the sake of example. In reality, a person might type in the numbers signifying a coin that was purchased earlier. The code for the interaction between the person and the coin machine is deliberately simplified. It doesn't do a good job of planning for failures in connections.

Notice that this section uses a different password to initialize the hash function ("It takes my dollar and my dream.") While that is close to the password used to create the coins, it is different enough to make it impossible for someone else to try to counterfeit coins with it.

8.2.3   Testing Winners

When a winner appears, the lottery department must check to see whether the ticket is valid. Here's the code for checking to confirm that everything is consistent. If the bettor isn't cheating, then $h(name, password)$ and $h(name,-password, numbers)$ can be found in `lottery`. The coin will also include a valid signature.

```java
public void testBet(String name,
                              String password,
                              int p1, int p2,
                              int p3, int p4,
                              int p5, int p6){

  MD5Bean.clear();
  MD5Bean.Update("It takes my dollar and my dream.");
  MD5Bean.Update(name);
  MD5Bean.Update(password);
  String idHash=MD5Bean.asHex();

  MD5Bean.clear();
  MD5Bean.Update("It takes my dollar and my dream.");
  MD5Bean.Update(name);
  MD5Bean.Update(password);

  MD5Bean.Update(""+p1+p2+p3+p4+p5+p6);
  String picks=MD5Bean.asHex();

  try{
    String qu="SELECT * FROM lottery WHERE name="+idHash+";";
    ResultSet rs=dw.executeQuery(qu);
    if (rs.next()){
      String picks2=rs.getString("picks");
      int coinNum=rs.getInt("coinNum");
      String coinSig=rs.getString("coinSig");
      MD5Bean.clear();
      MD5Bean.Update("Serial Num:"+coinNum);
      MD5Bean.Update("It takes a dollar and a dream.");
      String sig2=MD5Bean.asHex();

      if ((picks2.equals(picks)) && (sig2.equals(coinSig))){
        System.out.println("Ticket exists with valid coin.");
      } else {
        System.out.println("Ticket is good, but coin is bad.");
      }
    } else {
      System.out.println("Winning ticket is not found.");
    }
  } catch (SQLException e){
    System.out.println("SQL Exception:"+e);
  }
}
```

That code can be run only by the lottery office because it contains the secret phrase, "It takes a dollar and a dream," used as part of the MD-5 coin signing. Any curious person auditing the process can still run similar code and check to verify that $h(name, password)$ and $h(name, password, numbers)$ is in `lottery`.

The lottery management company might police the lottery with that function alone. There would be no need to test all the entries in `lottery` because there would be no incentive to invent fake coins if the lottery paid out for only valid choices. Of course, the lottery should check to see that the column `coinNum` doesn't contain copies produced by people trying to spend their coins two, three or n times.

A more vigilant lottery company may choose to check all the coins to see whether they're valid. Extra checking doesn't hurt, but it's not needed.

Here's a quick example:

```
Lottery l=new Lottery();
l.init();
l.makeBet("Harrison Jones","swordfish",2,3,5,7,11,13);
l.makeBet("Constance Harvey","lazy Sunday",7,11,13,19,26,31);
```

It produces these tables:

idNum	dateSold	dateRedeemed
-902156937	20011205101101	20011205101101
1367500165	20011205101101	20011205101101

name	picks	coinNum	coinSig
3894b6...	b7872f...	-902156937	eae5c3...
ca6f6b...	e4aa27...	1367500165	92d095...

The values of `dateSold` and `dateRedeemed` are the same because they're set when the coin is issued. There was no other code executed to mark them redeemed.

8.3 Sports Poker and Multiple Columns

There are times when several columns must be hidden in a database and then selectively revealed. The owner of the information may not want to show all the columns for any one of a number of reasons. Yet the rules of the game might require everyone to lock in all their information at the beginning. This section extends the strategy used throughout this chapter to multiple columns with multiple pieces of information.

There are many practical examples of when such a strategy could be needed. Revealing the least amount of information necessary is a common way to prevent fraud and deter criminals. You might show your age to the Social Security office to claim retirement funds at 65 while keeping that information secret from stores. Binding together multiple columns creates special identification cards that let you reveal some parts of the information but not others.

Section 8.4 explores an example with identity cards. This section focuses on using the techniques to create a type of sports-based poker. The game is a hybrid of regular sports betting and poker. I it invented just to illustrate the algorithms. It may be somewhat synthetic, but it is not without some charms. The game itself may be illegal in many parts of the world if you play it for real money so you might be careful with the code.

The game is similar to regular poker, but it uses your game predictions instead of cards. If you pick Washington over Saint Louis and Washington wins, then you've dealt yourself a good card. If you pick wrong, well, the value of your hand decreases. The details of which games to choose and how to pick a point spread are left out of this description because they aren't important for understanding how to create the game with a translucent database on the Internet. You're welcome to experiment.

Each player locks in predictions before the start of the day. Then there are several betting rounds as the day unfolds and the various games meander to an end. At the end, everyone all players their predictions if they want to claim the pot. The one with the most correct predictions wins. The best predictions are used to break the tie. Again, the details are left out of this description.

Locking in predictions and then revealing them afterward is the job for the algorithms in this chapter. Passing the information through a one-way function and then publicly storing the results is a good way to enforce commitment. If someone wants to claim the pot, that person can reveal the predicationsm and everyone can recompute the one-way function to verify accuracy.

Here's the SQL database used in the example:

```
CREATE TABLE gamebase (name CHAR(32),pick1 CHAR(32), pick2
CHAR(32), pick3 CHAR(32), pick4 CHAR(32), master CHAR(32));
```

This example uses four predictions stored in pick1 through pick4. Other games may use more or less. The name is stored in name. The final column, master, is used for a master hash of all the predictions. It is computed by a central referee and added to the database when a row of predictions is inserted. The master signature prevents someone from sneaking into the database and changing answers.

8.3.1   Inserting Predictions

This example does not force the players to format their predictions in any standard way. The predictions are just strings that might read, "Dallas over Chicago with a spread of 7 or more" or "San Francisco Smashes NY by 5 runs or more." The predictions are just strings that are hashed together using MD5.

This Java code is run by the participant's machine. It takes the predictions, the name and the password and passes it through the one-way function. The results are bound together in a String, which can be passed to a server administering the database.

```
public String packPicks(String name, String password,
  String pick1,String pick2,
  String pick3,String pick4){
  StringBuffer ans=new StringBuffer();
```

```
MD5Bean.clear();
MD5Bean.Update(name+"/"+password);
ans.append(MD5Bean.asHex());
ans.append(',');

MD5Bean.clear();
MD5Bean.Update(name+"/"+password+"/"+pick1);
ans.append(MD5Bean.asHex());
ans.append(',');

MD5Bean.clear();
MD5Bean.Update(name+"/"+password+"/"+pick2);
ans.append(MD5Bean.asHex());
ans.append(',');

MD5Bean.clear();
MD5Bean.Update(name+"/"+password+"/"+pick3);
ans.append(MD5Bean.asHex());
ans.append(',');
MD5Bean.clear();
MD5Bean.Update(name+"/"+password+"/"+pick4);
ans.append(MD5Bean.asHex());

return ans.toString();
}
```

The code uses only one password. A better solution may be to use a different randomly generated password for each of the different predictions. Eventually, a winning hand must be revealed. Using different passwords makes it simple to show one prediction but not another.

In this example, one password may be enough. There is no enforced structure to the predictionsm so it would be difficult for someone to try to guess them. Imagine that you know someone's name and password. If you could guess that person's prediction, you could run it through MD5 and check the result against the database. That is unlikely in this example because the predictions vary widely.

That is more likely if all players are forced to format their predictions. "NYM-NYY-5-3" is one standard way of saying "New York Mets 5, New York Yankees 3". Someone with knowledge of the format could run through all possible reasonable combinations in a short amount of time.

Of course, people develop verbal ticks like "of course". Some people always use the verb "smash". Others prefer "crush". It may make sense for a serious version to use randomly chosen passwords for each prediction just to protect people from their verbal ruts.

The server receives the information from the participant in one big string. It must break it apart and insert it into the right columns. The server also computes its own digital signature or hash of the data and stores it in the `master` column. That is intended to prevent people from sneaking into the database and changing their entries. Only someone who knows the master password can create that signature.

```
PreparedStatement insert;
```

```
public void initPS(){
String q="INSERT INTO gamebase SET name=?,";
q=q+"pick1=?,pick2=?,pick3=?,pick4=?,master=?;";
insert=dw.createPreparedStatement(q);
}

public void insertPicks(String picks, String masterPassword){
try{
  MD5Bean.clear();
  MD5Bean.Update(masterPassword);

  int p1=0;
  int p2=picks.indexOf(',');
  String temp=picks.substring(p1,p2);
  insert.setString(1,temp);

  p1=p2+1;
  p2=picks.indexOf(',',p1);
  temp=picks.substring(p1,p2);
  MD5Bean.Update(temp);
  insert.setString(2,temp);

  p1=p2+1;
  p2=picks.indexOf(',',p1);
  temp=picks.substring(p1,p2);
  MD5Bean.Update(temp);
  insert.setString(3,temp);

  p1=p2+1;
  p2=picks.indexOf(',',p1);
  temp=picks.substring(p1,p2);
  MD5Bean.Update(temp);
  insert.setString(4,temp);

  p1=p2+1;
  p2=picks.length();
  temp=picks.substring(p1,p2);
  MD5Bean.Update(temp);
  insert.setString(5,temp);
  insert.setString(6,MD5Bean.asHex());
  insert.executeUpdate();
} catch (SQLException e){
  System.out.println("SQL Exception:"+e);
}
}
```

Here's a quick example created with this code:

```
GameFace gf=new GameFace();
gf.init();

String t=gf.packPicks("Harrison Jones","swordfish",
 "Miami Over Dallas, 32-14", "New York and Chicago, over 190 points",
 "Boston v. LA, 110-90","Baltimore over Cleveland, 35-10");
gf.insertPicks(t,"tomato");
t=gf.packPicks("Candace Harvey","nopassword",
 "New York and Chicago, under 170 points",
```

```
"Baltimore over Cleveland, 14-10","Boston v. LA, 70-90",
"Dallas over Miami, 24-14");
gf.insertPicks(t,"tomato");
```

Here is what's inside table `gamebase`. The information doesn't mean much, but it's provided out of habit.

Column	Player 1	Player 2
name	c724b51a95213119c376b54153d693e8	114443e129ca4659e1aa7e9ea330a84e
pick1	6fa2ecf80220b21a20be78982a30e4b7	c82bd2ecfd9e5e12b730828aa3a18750
pick2	ff440df0a3b68f221d88bf1ee326c980	9b7dda32d8cca79d0ea10b8fe8155ba9
pick3	6d13c35505009af4ff43dfada0ec69d0	c0d599fc55f5c3f135c684355abceb70
pick4	cfc6e3b728647e336c9918a765aa42a5	67bbaa42773f35a0d433d413f266b6e3
master	d642d3511b00afc7dfb39f8bd4b1b83e	1f37222a32c72d8ecb02f0ee7c488009

8.3.2 Testing and Verifying

Eventually, after all the rounds of betting and all the rounds of watching the games, the players must decide to show a winning hand or fold their cards. Poker players often avoid showing too much because it helps others figure out their strategy. This game gives people the choice of revealing all, some or none of their predictions.

There are two routines used for verifying the database. The first can check each row to make sure that it still conforms to the way it was when the game began. The central authority shows its password at the end of the game, and everyone can check the rows to confrm that the signature stored in `master` still certifies the rows.

The `testAll` function will look up a particular name and password combination to verify that the signature is valid. This might be run by the server periodically or by the players at the end of the day.

```
public void testAll(String nameID,String masterPassword){
  try{
    MD5Bean.clear();
    MD5Bean.Update(masterPassword);

    String qu="SELECT * FROM gamebase WHERE name='"+nameID+"';";
    ResultSet rs=dw.executeQuery(qu);
    rs.next(); // one only for now.
    String temp;
    for (int i=2;i<6;i++){
      temp=rs.getString(i);
      MD5Bean.Update(temp);
    }
    temp=rs.getString(6);
    String ans=MD5Bean.asHex();
    if (temp.equals(ans)){
      System.out.println("Good row with nameId="+nameID);
    } else {
      System.out.println("Problem with nameId="+nameID);
    }
  } catch (SQLException e){
```

```
      System.out.println("SQL Exception:"+e);
  }
}
```

The second kind of verification lets players reveal their names, passwords and predictions. The code in revealGamePick lets everyone test individual predictions. Once everyone shows their values, everyone can go and check the individual predictions to determine the winners.

The code in revealGamePick needs the prediction in pick.

```
public void revealGamePick(String name, String password,
            String pick, int number){
  try{
    MD5Bean.clear();
    MD5Bean.Update(name+"/"+password+"/"+pick);
    String ans=MD5Bean.asHex();

    MD5Bean.clear();
    MD5Bean.Update(name+"/"+password);
    String nameID=MD5Bean.asHex();

    String qu="SELECT * FROM gamebase WHERE name='"+nameID+"';";
    ResultSet rs=dw.executeQuery(qu);
    String temp =rs.getString(number+1);
    if (temp.equals(ans)){
      System.out.println("Successful verification of pick.");
    } else {
      System.out.println("Things don't line up.");
    }
  } catch (SQLException e){
    System.out.println("SQL Exception:"+e);
  }
}
```

8.4   Identity Cards and Selective Revelations

The example in Section 8.3 shows how to bind together multiple predictions or values, using MD5 as the one-way function. This solution is quite efficient and reliable. Another solution uses the public-key algorithms that depend upon the intractability of the discrete log problem. These offer novel ways to bind together multiple pieces of information in one big number.

Section 7.3 uses similar mathematics to share a secret with multiple databases.

Locking together multiple pieces of information is usually considered quite useful if the information will be used as a credential. Imagine that one big block of information acted as your driver's license by encapsulating your name, age, height, weight, photo and driving privileges. The algorithms in this chapter make it possible to show these tidbits piece by piece if you want. Binding them together into one package discourages people from sharing these digital credentials. One of the best ways to do that is to bind together the credit card number and authorizing signature together with the identity. You may give your mega-ID to someone but only at the risk that the person will be able to spend your money, too. Telling them the password to unlock the mega-ID would open a real Pandora's box.

This section offers an example of how to create a digital ID record for a translucent database by using a mechanism built around the discrete log. It is used in many cryptographic algorithms and even patented for some applications. In this case, the owner can reveal selective pieces of personal data without revealing all of them.

8.4.1 The Basic Mathematics

Chapter 12 uses the same mathematics in reverse and presents the identity card as a token to unlock the records.

This section uses arithmetic modulo a prime number, p. The strength of the algorithm depends upon the fact that no one has publicly described how to invert exponentiation when it is done modulo a prime number. That is, it is easy to take x, g and p and compute $g^x \bmod p$, but it is hard to take $g^x \bmod p$ and work backward to compute x.

Let $\{x_1, x_2, \ldots, x_n\}$ be a set of numbers that you want to control and unveil on your own terms. They may be game scores, like those used in Section 8.3. They may be personal information, like your birth year or your weight. They could be your credit card number.

Let $\{g_1, g_2, \ldots, g_n\}$ be a set of *generators*. These are values less than p that generate all values less than p when raised to a power. That is, given y, there exists some i such that $y = g^i \bmod p$.

The secret values of x_i can be bound together into one big bundle by computing:

$$h = g_1^{x_1} g_2^{x_2} \ldots g_n^{x_n} \bmod p.$$

(Notice that h here is a big integer, not a function.) This value acts like a credential or a certificate. The holder will be able to reveal any particular value of x_i to someone without showing any of the others.

Often, this big number h would be certified by someone else using a digital signature. A digital driver's license, for instance, might bundle together the usual information and then come with a digital signature of the state's department of motor vehicles. This example will just use the value as an index for a database table. It acts like $h(name, password)$ in the other examples where h is a function.

Revealing one value of x_i is not difficult. It is like public-key signature verification, described in Section 10.2.2. This value h is like a big public key, and the process of showing one number is the same as signing a document and revealing one value at the same time.

Let's assume that a woman named Alice wants to prove that she has an entry in the database and that this entry would make her old enough to drink legally in the United States. Here are the steps:

1. The value of h is in the database. The person who placed it there knows the values of $\{x_1, x_2, \ldots, x_n\}$. For the sake of simplicity, let's assume that Alice wants to reveal that $x_1 = 1979$, a birth year that would make her

older than 21 and thus eligible to drink. Alice presents her birth year, 1979, to the database software.

2. The database software produces a challenge, c, that may be either a random number less than p or the hash of some document.

3. The database software divides h by $g_1^{1979} \bmod p$ and sets that to be h'. The rest of this algorithm works much like the digital signature-verification process in Section 10.2.2. Once the value of $g_1^{1979} \bmod p$ is divided out of h, the rest uses h'.

4. Alice constructs $n - 1$ witnesses, $\{w_2, w_3, \ldots, w_n\}$.

5. Alice computes $W = g_2^{w_2} g_3^{w_3} \ldots g_n^{w_n} \bmod p$.

6. Alice computes $n - 1$ values of a response: $r_i = cx_i + w_i$.

7. Alice sends W and $\{r_2, r_3, \ldots, r_n\}$.

8. The database checks to see if $W \frac{h}{g_1^{1979}}^c = g_2^{r_2} g_3^{r_3} \ldots g_l^{r_l} \bmod p$. It should be equal to that because:

$$
\begin{aligned}
W(\frac{h}{g_1^{1979}})^c &= W(g_2^{x_2} g_3^{x_3} \ldots g_l^{x_l})^c \\
&= W(g_2^{cx_2} g_3^{cx_3} \ldots g_l^{cx_l}) \\
&= (g_2^{w_2} g_3^{w_3} \ldots g_l^{w_l})(g_2^{cx_2} g_3^{cx_3} \ldots g_l^{cx_l}) \\
&= (g_2^{cx_2+w_2} g_3^{cx_3+w_3} \ldots g_l^{cx_l+w_l}) \\
&= g_2^{r_2} g_3^{r_3} \ldots g_l^{r_l} \bmod p
\end{aligned}
$$

9. If everything makes sense, the database assumes that Alice has successfully revealed her birth year, 1979, without exposing any of the other secret values.

This is just a basic technique for showing one value. There are more complex versions that reveal multiple values at once, show that some of the values satisfy some set of linear equations ($4x_3 + 17x_9 = 14$) or even show that some of the values satisfy some Boolean combination of equations. [Bra95] The area is the subject of much active inquiry because it allows flexibility and control for both sides of a transaction. Someone like Alice can reveal just what she wants while the other side can be certain she's not lying.

The protocol also has other advantages. The steps for revealing information about yourself can't be repeated by an eavesdropper. Every time the algorithm is executed, a different value of c is chosen. Someone can't reuse the information because it won't be consistent.

The algorithm can also be tweaked to punish people who execute the algorithm too often. In this example, Alice chooses values of w_i at random. If she happens to reuse the same values a second time, any observer will be able to use the values of r_i and the different values of c to show all the different values of x_i. Some cryptographers use features/bugs like this to create digital cash. Each value of h can be spent once and only once. If someone spends it more than once, the person's identity will pop out. You can either use this feature for your own purposes or as a warning to make sure that all your Alices use a good random-number generator to pick their witnesses.

8.4.2   A Rental Car Example

Car rental agencies are one of the more amazing products of the information age. Nothing illustrates the power of credentials more than the ability to walk into a shack, show someone a piece or two of plastic with your picture and drive away in a car worth $20,000 or more. This trust is a direct product of the ability to track down people who damage the car or fail to pay. The computer databases may raise dangers of Big Brother-like surveillance and abuse, but they also offer seductive convenience.

A translucent database can reduce some of these dangers by hiding personal information. The clerks at the rental car agency won't be able to misuse their power to use the computer to extract information about their customers. Yet the company will have all the information it needs to verify a person's identity and credit card information.

Here's the SQL creating the table `car`:

```
CREATE TABLE car (license TEXT,dateOut TIMESTAMP,
dateExpected TIMESTAMP, dateBack TIMESTAMP, rate INT);
```

The personal information is stored in one big integer in `license`. The date the car leaves the lot, the date it's expected back and the time it actually returns are recorded in `dateOut`, `dateExpected` and `dateBack`. The cost per day can be found in `rate`.

8.4.3   The License

In this example, the driver's license is actually a bigger credential encapsulating all the information stored on a driver's license as well as several credit card numbers. Bundling all that information together gives a car rental shop everything it needs.

This code is pretty flexible. It accepts any number of pairs consisting of a tag and a value and stores them in a `Vector` called `licenseItems`.

```
public void init(){
 licenseItems=new Vector();
 p=new BigInteger(768, 5, ran );
 g=new BigInteger(760, 5, ran );
}

public BigInteger stringToBigInteger(String s){
```

```
MD5Bean.clear();
MD5Bean.Update("Take a slow boat to China.");
MD5Bean.Update(s);
byte[] hashedPass=MD5Bean.Final();
return new BigInteger(hashedPass);
}


public void addToLicense(String tag, String value){
  licenseItems.addElement(tag+"="+value);
}

public String getTag(String tag){
  String s;
  int terms=licenseItems.size();
  for (int i=0;i<terms;i++){
    s=(String)licenseItems.elementAt(i);
    if (s.indexOf(tag)==0) return s;
  }
  return null;
}
```

Each of these items can be converted into a BigInteger with the function stringToBigInteger. The function getLicenseAsInteger computes $g^{x_1} g^{x_2} \dots g^{x_n} \bmod p$ where x_i is computed by stringToBigInteger(licenseItems.elementAt(i)).

```
public BigInteger getLicenseAsInteger(){
  int count=licenseItems.size();
  BigInteger ans=BigInteger.valueOf(1);
  String s;
  for (int i=0;i<count;i++){
    s=(String)licenseItems.elementAt(i);
    ans=ans.multiply(g.modPow(stringToBigInteger(s),p)).mod(p);
  }
   return ans;
}
```

Here's some example code that creates a new license and adds some information about your name, address and credit cards.

```
License l=new License();
l.init();
l.addToLicense("name","Harrison Jones");
l.addToLicense("address","1313 Mockingbird Lane");
l.addToLicense("ss","012345678");
l.addToLicense("cc1","1512443244425515");
l.addToLicense("cc2","5512344123412342");
l.addToLicense("birthdate","01/01/1960");
l.addToLicense("height","72");
l.addToLicense("weight","200");
l.addToLicense("eyesight","20/60");
```

Here's the value of the license in all of its glory:

62587060558185301776060236109068356552066194341973419253861855019015771542186271337924731671497051499228790347644064895141400390687255694572707397315173417372894124702402584167217706232517006521719471823408681339886873886253017249

This example leaves out another part of the story. This license is probably accompanied by a digital signature from the department of motor vehicles or some other trusted entity. The license in this example may be produced by the rental car company itself after verifying a person's driver's license and credit cards. Preprocessing the information and bundling it into a big integer like this could be one step for issuing a gold card to frequent renters.

8.4.4 Proving Information

Anyone who holds the license must be ready to show information about it to the rental car agency. The easiest way to do that is to print out all the values stored in the `Vector licenseItems`. Of course, that reveals everything, and the information might be misused by a malicious clerk or database interloper.

Revealing the information one item at a time gives the owner more power. The mathematics from Section 8.4.1 can be encapsulated in one Java class called `Proof`. Anyone who holds the class can check the values of r_i, c and W to make sure that they are consistent.

Here's the code:

```
public class Proof {
  // The object of the proof. Show that x exists.
  BigInteger license;
  BigInteger workingLicense;
  // What is proven.
  String proofString;
  // The challenge.
  BigInteger c;
  // How many items.
  int terms;
  // The values of r.
  BigInteger[] r;
  // The value of g^w1.
  BigInteger W;
  // The parameters
  BigInteger p,g;


  public Proof(int t){
    terms=t;
    W= BigInteger.valueOf(1);
    r=new BigInteger[terms];
    for (int i=0;i<terms;i++){
      r[i]=null;
    }
  }
}
```

```
public void setLicense(BigInteger c){
  license=c;
  workingLicense= license.add(BigInteger.valueOf(0));
  // Clone hack.
}

public BigInteger getLicense(){
  return license;  }

 public void setProofString(String s){
  proofString+=s+"\n";    }

public void setChallenge(BigInteger chal){
  c=chal; }

public void setParameters(BigInteger pp,BigInteger gg){
  p=pp;
  g=gg;
}

public void addTerm(BigInteger x,BigInteger w,int i){
  BigInteger gw=g.modPow(w,p);
  W=W.multiply(gw).mod(p);
  r[i]=(c.multiply(x)).add(w);
}

public void addProofTerm(BigInteger x){
  BigInteger t=g.modPow(x,p).modInverse(p);
  workingLicense=workingLicense.multiply(t).mod(p);
}

public BigInteger generateLeft(){
  BigInteger ans=BigInteger.valueOf(1);
  for (int i=0;i<terms;i++){
    if (r[i]!=null){
      ans=ans.multiply(g.modPow(r[i],p)).mod(p);
    }
  }
  return ans;
}

public BigInteger generateRight(){
  return workingLicense.modPow(c,p).multiply(W).mod(p);
 }

public String toString(){
  StringBuffer ans=new StringBuffer();
  for (int i=0;i<terms;i++){
    ans.append("r["+i+"]="+r[i]+"\n");
  }
  ans.append("W="+W+"\n");
  ans.append("c="+c+"\n");
  ans.append("license="+license+"\n");
  ans.append("working="+workingLicense+"\n");
  return ans.toString();
}
}
```

The proof is built at first by adding all the basic values. The `setParameters` function fixes the values of g and p. The license itself is inserted with `setLicense`. The challenge is probably provided by the rental car company and fixed using `setChallenge`.

The values of g^{x_i} are incorporated in two different ways. If g^{x_i} corresponds to a part of the license that is *not* being revealed, then the method `addTerm` takes x_i, multiplies it by the challenge c and then adds in the value of w_i before storing the result in the array `r`. A random value of g^{w_i} is rolled into the value of W before the value of w_i is discarded.

If the value of x_i corresponds to a `tag` that is being shown, then it is divided out of the value of `workingLicense`. That is, h becomes $\frac{h}{g^{x_i} \bmod p}$. At the beginning, the value of `License` is the same as `workingLicense`.

The algorithms in this section can be extended to generate the licenses anonymously if needed. [Bra95]

Here's some code for creating a proof from a license. It begins by setting the parameters and then steps through the various tags in `licenseItems`. The tag being disclosed is recorded in the Proof in `setProofString`. This is largely to help anyone who receives a copy of `Proof` understand just what is being revealed.

```java
public Proof constructProof(BigInteger challenge,
                            String tag){
  // prove you know the right tag.
  int terms=licenseItems.size();
  Proof ans=new Proof(terms);
  ans.setChallenge(challenge);
  ans.setParameters(p,g);
  ans.setCert(getLicenseAsInteger());
  String s;
  for (int i=0;i<terms;i++){
    s=(String)licenseItems.elementAt(i);
    if (s.indexOf(tag)==0){
      ans.addProofTerm(stringToBigInteger(s));
      ans.setProofString(s);
    } else {
      ans.addTerm(stringToBigInteger(s),
          new BigInteger(760,ran).abs(),i);
    }
  }
  return ans;
}
```

Here's a proof generated with the `License` created for Harrison Jones up above:

variable	value
r[0]	null
r[1]	302207221627773243096434554641809636593075316317573556101391221989967706733023805455174275408538137297797742171531570956798020914604121560134894789758672188091217021373334302951811464102856981144541148206250200024599580545771189657486932536204053368836362100248808511
r[2]	110954797248001811682748535453986499364270395279991031815019745571608537932892420568960294697262814871730231145425022362170653796380790552882038205090080387554239699828430664293183860913350708102602544798676461478162018056453450416356318673054972132904827611377225136111
r[3]	119933623265707700164996071278429957771304527827142519509355467050875785723823283164096963621788914794990064535768863596533427552930993475605339880999666142593634459951088769524562074766128858956677060840288618330066831602551512125056080584773568510457841078862424639
r[4]	-295102128696297147386235988165684614428283666967015084268290998028930633670171157793398416034710571489553253722986274049172936173971622141758578249631170671166135492547674555975922389627340419515109248239999259733392558486994180951256834942823928302824187862138771597
r[5]	380345140490556159800079816534457885367914082587338171571528899491164835948801179143800840574695023706591694011648958004678686743118383621612486665397497751927008623359304602104276841788847303076882770020087931655548499288222786532192720653978617293672074760517474785
r[6]	234763863357220394973461840255514088273024293838001000400573690208970169708325398752852306541092400130631904726023151694581427463771480414350232936956009870199336716602215513166631680519631157344026505296019331350741858904850931527031444058041752279077957061465300721
r[7]	-393764826831840228606893275991966019671975412155259420849104080996665494191754278607067341954076953758265011295209896672724870184854633025871141482271645516588639195013239527660076791428004948280137888691450140838114013665797167169298800090630591364389931888271876771
r[8]	107756610002275130871143465742502898027156746743690324405687780061491887779661286497091239234565790602044365175297776698624451563794356924196633418925228314494355581916711004807852273201380960040831457720949852109884600678766152947805778327502615707735526703673321304
W	559710468391388040258271828002270784181184903408957215054779033149262697442600005861928463984607673483634790448148774170103259101492947693770607702581357639254299889177036272176838662696856970584054186857009012425690682736353345506
c	719088358008651629374089626117714687184654141301891394467276353273201496265804826889201326793175781361953374831497185212593057312659468918963650552739905175471402037905059736645812407589084591042277717897441204796781060817779718
license	600297435491833014227266648735041141161069702704909084489440224724874502685056678093147426327580584595145512998447923769373083692428030988238116653043958389847104958093108725973314066236600181635752194421152756429536451009735321983
workingL	41402953177586869993704304573609559353263720692301396597429581085114194080880141613447287194397604346922693818688607652676451126422306002054778263396029184627516510024607576451060165717895941545513610176869020311365878131863930861

The value of r[0] is null because this proof discloses the string "name=-Harrison Jones". The value of $g^{x_1} \bmod p$ was divided out of the value of workingLicense.

Anyone who received an object from the class Proof could check it using the methods generateLeft and generateRight. The first mixes together the values of r_i and computes $g^{r_1} g^{r_2} \ldots g^{r_n} \bmod p$, avoiding the values where r[i] is null. The function generateRight takes the license, raises it to the power of c and then multiplies it by W. These two values should be equal if the person who produced the object knew the correct values of x_i.

This code can also show multiple lines at the same time. There's no reason why several values of r[i] can't end up as null. Someone revealing a name and birthday in the same transaction can bundle them together in one object.

8.4.5   The Rental Car Company

This example does not explore the many ways that the rental car company can use the information provided by the license holder. Most rental car companies ask car renters to provide proof that they hold valid licenses and credit card s*before* the cars leave the lot. This example asks them to disclose only their names. It assumes that if a license is valid, the credit card numbers buried within it must be good. That may be correct in some cases but wrong in others. A real working version calls for more attention to customer service, fraud prevention and risk management.

Here are two methods that are used to check out a car and accept it back when it returns. In the first, `rentCar`, the renter discloses a name. In the second, the renter unveils a credit card number used to pay for the trip. Both accept a `Proof` object created by the renter.

```
public void rentCar(Proof nameProof,
                    java.util.Date dateBack){
  try{
    System.out.println("Proof with tag:"+nameProof.proofString);
    if (nameProof.generateLeft().equals(nameProof.generateRight())){
      insert.setString(1,nameProof.getCert().toString());
      java.util.Date dd=new java.util.Date().getTime());
      insert.setTimestamp(2,new java.sql.Timestamp(dd);
      insert.setTimestamp(3,new java.sql.Timestamp(dateBack.getTime()));
      insert.setInt(5,30);
      insert.executeUpdate();
    } else {
      System.out.println("I'm sorry your license isn't valid.");
    }
  } catch (SQLException e){
    System.out.println("SQL Exception:"+e);
  }
}

public void returnCar(Proof ccProof){
  try{
    System.out.println("Proof with tag:"+ccProof.proofString);
    String q="SELECT * FROM car WHERE license='"+ccProof.getCert()+"';";
    ResultSet rs=dw.executeQuery(q);
    if (rs.next()){
      if (ccProof.generateLeft().equals(ccProof.generateRight())){
      /// Charge the credit card presented.
      }
    }
  } catch (SQLException e){
    System.out.println("SQL Exception:"+e);
  }
}
```

This code can check that the proof provided is correct by comparing the results of `generateLeft` and `generateRight`. If they're equal, the car company knows that the right information was revealed with the license.

8.5 Conclusions

There are two basic tricks for showing some information stored in a translucent database. The first is to unveil it, bits and all. If the translucent database is hiding the information by applying a one-way function, then anyone can find the right row by applying the one-way function again to the information unveiled.

The second mechanism works with public-key algorithms. Instead of revealing the information itself, the owners of the information can make a few basic calculations using a random number provided as a challenge. The values that come out do not show the information itself but are structured in such a way that the values be unveiled only by someone who knows the data itself.

Both the public-key and the regular one-way functions can be applied to multiple fields and the owner of the data can show different fields at different times.

8.5.1 Lessons

- If the databases hold $h(x)$, the people who know x can later reveal it to claim.

- Public-key algorithms let you prove you know x without showing it.

- Public-key algorithms use a different value, known as the challenge, or c during each proof of knowledge. If the database generates a different c, then an eavesdropper cannot reuse any old recorded information.

- Finding rows with public-key algorithms can be very time-consuming if the proof is tested against every value of $h(x)$.

- Looking up information can be accelerated dramatically if the prover offers both the value of $h(x)$ and the values documenting the knowledge of x. The value of $h(x)$ finds the right row to test the proof. The downside is that the prover must reveal $h(x)$ over the wire. An eavesdropper could combine that information with access to the database to find the right record.

- Multiple fields can be combined with a one-way function. That is, store $h(x_1)$, $h(x_2)$, $h(x_3)$, and $h(h(x_1)h(x_2)h(x_3))$.

- Multiple fields can be combined into one large integer with the public-key algorithms.

- Binding together multiple credentials discourages cheating. Someone may be less likely to lend someone a driver's license if the license also includes a copy of the owner's credit card number and the ability to approve payment.

- These schemes are used by others as anonymous credentials, digital cash tools, or anonymous voting booths.

Chapter 9

Quantization

Translucent databases are tools for giving some people enough access to the data to do their work without giving them too much access. If perfect precision is not necessary, rounding off the data is one simple solution. If the marketing department compares buying patterns with postal codes, then throw away the street addresses but not the postal codes. Keeping the minimal amount of information is a good way to add security and save money on disk space.

Many mathematicians often use the term *quantization* to refer to the larger problem of rounding off data. The algorithms break the space into a set of *quanta* and then match each data point with a particular quantum. Rounding off real numbers is equivalent to creating quanta $i - .5 \leq x < i + .5$ for all integers, i. Each value is assigned to the closest integer, which lies in the center of its quantum.

More complex algorithms don't break up the data space into equal parts. Sometimes large quanta make sense if that corner of the data space is used rarely. Sometimes small quanta make sense if detail is important. Some algorithms mix and match these.

In an ideal application, quantized information can be used successfully without revealing anything about the protected information. Some medical researchers, for instance, seek to ensure that each quantum includes at least five different people. A rural road with just one family of four would not be large enough to act as a quantum. Any release of the data could not include the road name because that would be enough information to focus on four people. If the medical researchers wanted to share that information, they might give only the city or county of those residents, not their street. In a bigger city, however, the floor of an apartment building might hold more than 100 people, and sharing such information would not focus too much on one person.

Not all quantization deals with individuals. The military may want to show a unit's latitude and longitude in degrees but leave out the minutes and seconds. An agent may want to brag that a contract is a "six-figure contract" without specifying whether it is for $100,000 or $999,999. Categorizing data using quanta is a common shorthand for everyone, not just database designers seeking security.

Sometimes quantization doesn't really deal with precision at all. Many companies store only the first four or the last four digits of a credit card number. Others store only the last four digits of a Social Security number. That acts like a one-way function for identifying the credit card or the Social Security number. The owner of the right number can match the four digits, but an attacker can't do much with just the last four digits.

Aleksander Ohrn and Lucila Ohno-Machado use boolean reasoning to delete only the data that would allow deducing a person's identity.[OOM99]

Here are the basic techniques:

Rounding Split the real numbers into equal units. Some common sizes are units of length 10^i for physical units and 2^i in the digital realm.

Logarithmic Rounding Round off the log of the number instead of the number itself. We often use units of three: thousands, millions, billions, trillions, etc.

Deleting Smaller Fields Instead of storing the day, hour, minute and second, store just the day. Instead of storing the apartment number, street address, city, state and ZIP, store only the city and state.

Add Random Amounts Adding a random amount of information to the data is technically not quantizing it, but it has a similar effect. It reduces the most precise details to noise. It may not zero out the smallest fields, but it has the same effect.

In the past, the military added random amounts to the coordinates returned by the Global Positioning System to prevent enemies from using it to aim missiles. The system was capable to providing a location within a few feet, but the extra random error meant that it was accurate to within only hundreds of feet. The military recently shut off tha feature after civilian use became widespread.

Projection A shadow is a two-dimensional projection of a three-dimensional object. Some information is lost, but other information remains. Projecting some n dimensional data into some smaller space is an easy way to reduce information in a mathematically rigorous way.

You can think of deleting smaller fields as projection. Dropping the seconds field from a time removes one dimension. Dropping the minutes field loses another dimension.

The real challenge is projecting the data when there are no obvious fields to drop. The challenge is to find the best angle for viewing the data.

There are probably a few more techniques for reducing the information kept around in databases. All of them are powerful techniques for building translucent databases that provide enough precision to do some work without providing enough precision to misuse the information.

9.1 Algorithms

Many algorithms for data minimization and quantization are simple. If you don't want to keep the extra fields, don't store them. If the information is already in the database table, then you can just DELETE them with an ALTER TABLE command. Rounding off numbers is also simple, and many computer languages come with built-in commands to do it. Even adding random amounts is not much of a challenge. Just make sure that the random amounts are small enough to avoid destroying the bigger details.

A greater challenge is coming up with optimal schemes for quantizing information or projecting it. This approach is as much a science as an art, and each algorithm may do well in some cases while performing poorly in others.

Latanya Sweeney created the SCRUBS and Datafly systems to show how quantization can protect medical records. [Swe96][Swe97][SS00]

9.1.1 Adaptive Quantization

Adaptive quantization schemes are used frequently in compression algorithms, especially with digitized images. The amount of red, blue and green in the color of each pixel is usually specified with three bytes or 24 bits. Artists and photographers often like that precision, but many are quite happy with smaller files that take up less bandwidth. This is really a problem of taking a three-dimensional space and finding a set of quanta that best represent it.

The GIF image format, for instance, saves space by choosing a subset of 2^i colors and then replacing each pixel with one of these colors. If we assume that $i = 8$, as it often is, then each pixel takes only 8 bits instead of 24, but there are only 256 total colors instead of billions. The challenge is to pick those 256 so the distortion is minimal.

There are many schemes for choosing the set of colors to represent all other colors. Some try to group similar colors, while others try to split the space into areas of equal size. Others try to take into consideration the sensitivity of the average eye to changes in red, green and blue.

The process winds up with something that can be compared to the United States Congress, where 535 people represent the population as a whole. In one half, the House of Representatives, the positions are distributed according to population. The island of Manhattan, for instance, gets several, while the state of Wyoming gets only one. The other half, the Senate, gives each state two positions.

I quite agree with you. The sun is not kind. God should use a rose amber spot.
–Dewitt Bodeen
Curse of the Cat People

The first approach, the one used by the House of Representatives, concentrates the most quanta where most of the data happens to be. If most of the colors in an image happen to be concentrated in the pinks, then there will be many tiny quanta representing the different shades of pink. That solution preserves plenty of detail by concentrating it where it can do the most good, but it often does a poor job representing a minority of the colors. Big areas of the color cube are often lumped together, maybe placing blues, greens and oranges together in one quantum. That can lead to ghastly compressed images in which all the blues, greens and oranges are replaced by one color, say,

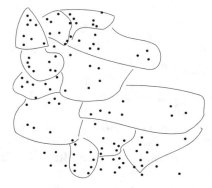

Figure 9.1: A set of points in two-dimensions divided into quanta by choosing points at random and then lumping the closest points together. This works well for many points, but leaves outlying points to be gathered into the last remaining quanta.

green. Although there may not be many pixels in this, the big change can really stick out.

Here's a basic algorithm for that type of approach. Let there be m colors. The job is to reduce m to 256.

1. Choose a pixel at random.

2. Find the closest $\frac{m}{256}$ colors.

3. Toss them into one quantum and remove them from the set.

4. Repeat until there are only 256 colors.

The distance between two colors can be measured with the simple metric: $(r_1 - r_2)^2 + (g_1 - g_2)^2 + (b_1 - b_2)^2$, where (r_1, b_1, g_1) and (r_2, b_2, g_2) are the red, blue and green coordinates of the two pixels. Better metrics try to weight the differences to account for the way the human eye responds to red, blue and green. It is also possible to weight this process by the number of pixels in each particular color.

This random approach is far from perfect. Many points chosen at the beginning will end up in appropriate quanta, but some of the outlying points scattered around the edges will also be lumped together at the end. The points in the corners will end up bunched together. Figure 9.1 shows how a few unmatched points are left out of quanta.

A better solution is to choose a different threshold than $\frac{m}{256}$. If only, say, 90% of the points are distributed by this process, then the remaining 10% can be allocated to the closest quantum. This removes the problem of lumping together the stray points. Using a threshold of $\frac{.9m}{256}$ accomplishes this.

The second approach is a bit more complicated but can lead to fewer distortions. It is closer in spirit to the way the Senate fills its chambers. The algorithm begins with all the colors in one three-dimensional box and divides the space into smaller boxes until there are 256 boxes. At each step, the biggest box with the greatest diversity in color is the one that's divided.

The mechanism for choosing the box to subdivide and then subdividing it is also an art. Here's one solution for choosing the box to subdivide.

1. For each box, find the greatest difference in red values. That is, find the two colors in the box with the greatest difference in their red components.

2. For each box, find the greatest difference in green values.

3. For each box, find the greatest difference in blue values.

4. Now find the biggest difference over all boxes and all colors.

5. Split that box in half along the axis of the greatest difference.

That process begins with one three-dimensional cube and ends with 256 different rectangular solids.

There are several different ways to approach splitting the box. Let one corner be (r_1, g_1, b_1) and the other be (r_2, g_2, b_2). Assume the red color is the axis with the greatest difference in values. Here are some solutions:

- Split the box using the box's coordinates alone. That is, split this box in half at $r = \frac{(r_2 - r_1)}{2}$. That increases the size of the box, but it could easily leave one new half-box with no colors in it at all.

- Split the box at the median of all red values in the box. That is guaranteed to avoid leaving an empty box, but it can create very small boxes if the colors are clustered in one corner. It guarantees, though, that half of the colors will end up in one box and half in the other.

- Split the box at the average of the red values in the box. That also creates thin boxes if the colors are clustered in one corner, but it does not ensure that half will end up in each box.

After 256 boxes emerge from the algorithm, one color must be chosen to represent each box. The simplest solution is to pick the geometrical center of the box. Another is to average all the colors in the box. A third is to pick one of the colors at random. Either of the first two are good solutions for picking the value to represent the quanta.

Figure 9.2 shows how this algorithm would allocate the same two-dimensional set of points from Figure 9.1. In this case, the points are placed in one big two dimensional box at the beginning. At each step, the box with the greatest "pointspread" is split into four smaller boxes. This continues until enough quanta are produced. Then, the points are replaced by the average

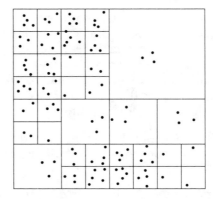

Figure 9.2: The same two-dimensional set of points from Figure 9.1 are allocated into quanta by splitting apart the quanta. At each step, one box with the greatest dispersion of points is split into four smaller boxes. The result is that each box holds tightly packed points.

of the points in their particular quantum. There are no large quanta with widespread points produced by this algorithm, although sometimes many points are clustered together in one box.

That solution generally produces better colors with fewer gross differences between the actual color and its quantized value. Large boxes are broken up, even if they have only a few scattered colors. Only one quantum replaces tight clusters of many colors, even if there are many, many colors in that cluster.

That approach generally does a better job of covering vast spaces and minimizing the differences in each quantum.

While this example is drawn from the task of quantizing color spaces, there is no reason the algorithms can't be applied to all other data spaces. The goal is to find surrogates for the vast number of items. Good surrogates will provide functional replacements for the data points in the quantum and provide some security for the data. Replacing the data points with the new information shields the data inside.

9.1.2 Projection

Many people use the word *projection* to refer to converting data to fit into a new, often smaller, space. Making shadow puppets on the wall with your hands is a projection that takes the three-dimensional world of your hands and converts it into the two-dimensional space of the wall.

Figure 9.3 shows how problematic this process can be. The figure shows two vectors in two different orientations and the result of projecting them onto a one-dimensional space directly below them. In one, the two vectors end up pointing in different directions. In the other, they end up being almost

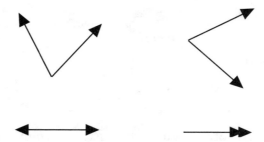

Figure 9.3: The top half of this figure shows two views of a pair of lines in two dimensions. The bottom half shows their projection into one horizontal dimension. The same lines create very different views if they are placed at different orientations. Choosing the right angle of orientation can be an art form that controls the perception of the data.

exactly the same.

There is no easy way to choose the "best" projection for each collection of data. In some sense, it is an art as much as a science. Anyone can choose the angle that best conveys the information the person wants to project.

Figure 9.4 shows how the software package Spindoctor takes a collection of random data in 20 dimensions and projects it, first down into three dimensions and then down into two. It uses the singular value decomposition to find the best angle to use to create a three-dimensional version of the data. The user can rotate the object around three different axes to get a better feeling for which points are near others.

The *singular value decomposition* is an algorithm used in matrix algebra. The process is closely connected to finding the eigenvalues and eigenvectors of a matrix, two tasks that are commonly used in physics and engineering. The largest singular values correspond to the best direction for viewing the data. The Spindoctor software chooses the three largest singular values and discards the rest. The size of the discarded values is used to compute the potential error in the projection.

To be more exact, let M be a matrix with the data. A singular value decomposition finds two orthogonal matrices, U and V, such that $M = UDV^t$ where D is a diagonal matrix with the singular values arranged along the diagonal. The singular values are usually arranged from largest to smallest along the diagonal, with the largest in the upper-left-hand corner.

The matrix U is a rotation matrix which means that it is effectively finding the best position for viewing of the data in M. Spindoctor sets all but the top three singular values in D to be zero. The result, DV^t, effectively reduces the data in M to three dimensions. The number of zeros replacing the singular values controls the size of the projection. That is, to keep three dimensions, replace all but the largest three singular values in D with zeros. To keep four dimensions, replace all except the largest four singular values in D with zeros.

This Henry Emery Person, our Person's father, might be described as a well-meaning, earnest, dear little man, or as a wretched fraud, depending on the angle of light and the position of the observer.
–Vladimir Nabokov
Transparent Things

Gene Golub and Charles van Loan's book, Matrix Computations, *is a good introduction to the mathematics of working with matrices on computers.*

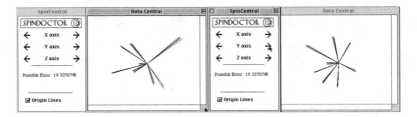

Figure 9.4: Two views of the same eight clusters of points in 20 dimensions. The software, Spindoctor, uses the singular value decomposition to find the best angle for projecting the data into three dimensions. The user can rotate the object and find the best angle to project the points down into two dimensions.

An estimate of the amount of potential error can be found by determining the size of the excluded singular value.

9.2   Using Quantization In Databases

The simplest way to use quantization with a database is to apply the algorithm and throw away the unwanted detail. If you've chosen the parameters correctly, the lack of detail should be enough to confound any attacker looking in the database.

There are a few more complex solutions that scramble the data in ways that let some people have access to the precision while leaving others outside. The data can be encrypted so only those with the right password can find it.

Here's an example built around naval ships. During peacetime, the U.S. Navy may want to let general information about a ship's position circulate because it makes life easier in many ways. Crew members can communicate with loved ones, who may want to follow their path around the globe. Rendezvous with suppliers and civilian ships can be planned. People from other parts of the armed forces can make plans without sending a request through a complicated classified bureaucracy. Making the general position public is a good idea if it can be done without providing enough information to make an attack easy.

For the sake of simplicity, let's assume that there's little threat in describing the latitude and longitude of the ship in degrees as long as there's no mention of the minutes and seconds. In practice, the Navy may want to use greater or smaller distances.

Here's an SQL command for creating a database:

```
CREATE TABLE navy1 (ship TINYTEXT, latitudeD TINYINT,
latitudeM TINYINT, latitudeS TINYINT, longitudeD TINYINT,
longitudeM TINYINT, longitudeS TINYINT);
```

The ship's name is stored in `ship`, and the degrees, minutes and seconds of latitude could end up in `latitudeD`, `latitudeM` and `latitudeS` if the values are stored with full precision. The longitude is stored in `longitudeD`, `longitudeM` and `longitudeS`.

Here's some Java code for initializing the connection to the database:

```
MD5 MD5Bean=new MD5();
java.util.Random ran;
DatabaseWrapper dw=new DatabaseWrapper();
public void init(){
  dw.init();
  ran=new java.util.Random();
  initAppointments1();
}
PreparedStatement navyInsert,lookup;
public void initAppointments1(){
  String q="INSERT INTO navy1 SET ship=?,";
  q=q+"latitudeD=?,latitudeM=?,latitudeS=?,";
  q=q+"longitudeD=?,longitudeM=?,longitudeS=?;";
  navyInsert=dw.createPreparedStatement(q);
}
```

The `PreparedStatement`, `navyInsert`, will add data reporting the position.

9.2.1 Adding Random Noise

Sometimes replacing the extra detail with zeros makes sense. It can show that the extra precision is not available and that anyone trusting the data should not assume that the ship is exactly at a position where the minutes and seconds are zero.

In other cases, adding random noise helps obscure the position. The table `navy1` may hold the real positions of ships in dry dock or at ceremonial functions but obscure the positions of those on active duty. Therefore, a set of four zeros would show which ships were on active duty.

Here's some code that finds a random permutation and adds it to the values:

```
public void randomInsert(String ship,
                         int lad, int lam, int las,
                         int lod, int lom, int los){
  try {
    navyInsert.setString(1,ship);
    navyInsert.setInt(2,lad);
    navyInsert.setInt(5,lod);    int
    temp=Math.abs(lam+ran.nextInt()) % 60;
    navyInsert.setInt(3,temp);
    temp=Math.abs(las+ran.nextInt()) % 60;
    navyInsert.setInt(4,temp);
    temp=Math.abs(lom+ran.nextInt()) % 60;
    navyInsert.setInt(6,temp);
    temp=Math.abs(los+ran.nextInt()) % 60;
    navyInsert.setInt(7,temp);
    navyInsert.executeUpdate();
  } catch (SQLException e){
```

```
    System.out.println("SQL Exception:"+e);
  }
}
```

This is a pretty basic solution. The random numbers are probably much larger than 60, the limit for minutes and seconds. So it effectively replaces the fields containing the minutes and seconds with random values.

A better solution might calculate a random value within a circle of a fixed radius of δ. If that is added to the values, then the position of the ship would always be accurate to within δ.

9.2.2   Adding Encryption

One simple solution is to use a built-in encryption function like MySQL's ENCODE function. The data can be stored with SQL commands like:

```
INSERT INTO navy1 VALUES("USS Enterprise",
48,ENCODE(15,'swordfish'),ENCODE(50,'swordfish'),
52,ENCODE(40,'swordfish'),ENCODE(50,'swordfish'));
```

The one problem is that this command won't work. The ENCODE function returns a larger string of information that must be stored in a BLOB field. That makes it impractical to store encrypted and unencrypted information in the same table.

A better solution is to create an encrypted amount of noise and add that to the position. This allows the precision to be restored by subtracting the same noise.

Here's some Java code that uses an MD5 hash to build a random permutation. The function computes $h(\text{"Beat Army!"}, passcode, ship)$ and uses four of the bytes to permute the values in the minutes and seconds.

```
public int scrambleValue(int in, byte b){
   return (in +Math.abs(b % 60))%60;
 }

 public void encryptedInsert(String passcode,String ship,
                      int lad, int lam, int las,
                           int lod,int lom, int los){
 try {
   // take care of unencrypted first.
   navyInsert.setString(1,ship);
   navyInsert.setInt(2,lad);
   navyInsert.setInt(5,lod);

   // Find encryption key

   MD5Bean.clear();
   MD5Bean.Update("Beat Army!");
   MD5Bean.Update(passcode+ship);
   byte[] b=MD5Bean.Final();

   int temp=scrambleValue(lam,b[0]);
```

```
navyInsert.setInt(3,temp);
temp=scrambleValue(las,b[1]);
navyInsert.setInt(4,temp);
temp=scrambleValue(lom,b[2]);
navyInsert.setInt(6,temp);
temp=scrambleValue(los,b[3]);
navyInsert.setInt(7,temp);

navyInsert.executeUpdate();
} catch (SQLException e){
System.out.println("SQL Exception:"+e);
}
}
```

Here's the result of adding two ships to the database. The minutes and seconds are scrambled to prevent detection.

ship	latitudeD	latitudeM	latitudeS	longitudeD	longitudeM	longitudeS
USS Enterprise	48	14	30	50	25	56
USS Nimitz	22	8	55	30	20	33

Anyone who knows the `passcode` can unscramble values by reversing the process. That allows everyone to use the public database, including the people with access to the greater detail protected by `passcode`.

```
public int unscrambleValue(int in, byte b){
    int i=in-Math.abs(b%60);
  if (i<0) i+=60;
  return i;
}

public void findShip(String ship, String passcode){
 try{
    String qu="SELECT * FROM navy1 WHERE ship='"+ship+"';";
    ResultSet rs=dw.executeQuery(qu);
    rs.next();// first one only.
    int lad=rs.getInt(2);
    int lam=rs.getInt(3);
    int las=rs.getInt(4);
    int lod=rs.getInt(5);
    int lom=rs.getInt(6);
    int los=rs.getInt(7);

    // Find encryption key

    MD5Bean.clear();
    MD5Bean.Update("Beat Army!");
    MD5Bean.Update(passcode+ship);
    byte[] b=MD5Bean.Final();

    lam=unscrambleValue(lam,b[0]);
    las=unscrambleValue(las,b[1]);
    lom=unscrambleValue(lom,b[2]);
    los=unscrambleValue(los,b[3]);

    String pos=ship+" is at ("+lad+":"+lam+":"+las;
    pos+=","+lod+":"+lom+":"+los+")";
```

```
  System.out.println(pos);
  } catch (SQLException e){
    System.out.println("SQL Exception:"+e);
  }
}
```

9.3   Quantized One-Way Functions

Pure encryption is not the only way to deal with quantized data. One-way functions provide just as much scrambling, but none of the ability to recover the information (unless you use a public-key function). That scrambling can still provide useful databases that protect the identities of individuals. Applying a one-way function to the precision blocks access to the data without obscuring some of the data analysis.

Consider this example of a scientific study of the correlation between smoking, radon gas and lung cancer. The database contains a list of people, their addresses, their smoking habits, the amount of radon in their houses, and the prevalence of cancer.

Here's the SQL line for initializing the table:

```
CREATE TABLE radon1 (nameID CHAR(32), stNum INT, aptNum INT,
   street CHAR(40), zip INT, radon INT, smoke INT, cancer INT);
```

For the sake of illustration, we'll assume that the smoking habits (smoke), the radon concentration (radon) and the occurrence of cancer (cancer) can be summarized with an integer. The address data and the amount of quantization in it is our real concern. The street number (stNum) and apartment number (aptNum) are left as integers. The street name (street) itself could be stored in the clear or as the aftermath of a one-way function. The ZIP code, zip, is left in the clear to allow analysis.

Here are four lines inserting data into the table:

```
INSERT INTO radon1 VALUES(MD5("Herman
Munster"),1313,null,MD5("Mockingbird Lane"),90210,4,5,3);

INSERT INTO radon1 VALUES(MD5("Jackson
Smith"),1315,null,MD5("Mockingbird Lane"),90210,2,15,3);

INSERT INTO radon1 VALUES(MD5("Carrie
O'Donnovan"),1317,null,MD5("Mockingbird Lane"),90210,4,4,2);

INSERT INTO radon1 VALUES(MD5("Caroline
O'Rourke"),1319,null,MD5("Mockingbird Lane"),90210,1,7,3);
```

The data ends up looking like this:

nameID	stNum	street	zip	radon	smoke	cancer
92c81c...	1313	4d1c...	90210	4	5	3
128b6d...	1315	4d1c...	90210	2	15	3
bdb9af...	1317	4d1c...	90210	4	4	2
42178d...	1319	4d1c...	90210	1	7	3

The researchers studying this database can examine many different correlations between radon, smoking and cancer. They can look at geographic effects, something that may be useful because radon can depend on geology. Everyone living on the same street has the same value of $h(street)$ so the correlations between neighbors can be studied.

The personal information, though, is obscured by the translucency. The researchers do not need to worry about showing sensitive information about cancer because the names and the streets are obscured through the MD5 hash function. Anyone who tries to guess information about someone using a street name will not get very far. The researchers can be sure that even in rural areas with low population density, there won't be enough information to identify a person associated with a particular radon/smoking/cancer score.

If the street-level information is not needed by the researchers, then the numbers can be added to the hash function. Each house will have a different value:

```
INSERT INTO radon1 VALUES(MD5("Herman
Munster"),null,null,MD5("1313 Mockingbird
Lane"),90210,4,5,3);

INSERT INTO radon1 VALUES(MD5("Jackson
Smith"),null,null,MD5("1315 Mockingbird
Lane"),90210,2,15,3);

INSERT INTO radon1 VALUES(MD5("Carrie
O'Donnovan"),null,null,MD5("1317 Mockingbird
Lane"),90210,4,4,2);

INSERT INTO radon1 VALUES(MD5("Caroline
O'Rourke"),null,null,MD5("1319 Mockingbird
Lane"),90210,1,7,3);
```

This table looks like:

nameID	street	zip	radon	smoke	cancer
92c81c...	447bc1...	90210	4	5	3
128b6d...	09e5e6...	90210	2	15	3
bdb9af...	c7e698...	90210	4	4	2
42178d...	3c15b0...	90210	1	7	3

The translucency and the hash functions have limits. If you know the name, you can look up the record. If you know the street name, you can pass it through the hash function and examine the records of everyone on the street. A more secure example would include a password in the data fed to the MD5. That would probably be a studywide password known to all the researchers. Casual browsers, hackers and other interlopers wouldn't know the password and thus wouldn't be able to look up people by name or street.

```
INSERT INTO radon1 VALUES(MD5(''swordfish/Herman
Munster"),1313,null, MD5("tomato/Mockingbird
Lane"),90210,4,5,3);
```

This weakness is also a feature for many scientific studies. If the team is able to gather new information each year, it can still update the database. Every time new information about a house on Mockingbird Lane arrives, the team can apply the one-way function, find the correct record and update it. The data is protected in the interim from casual analysis, but it can be changed later.

9.3.1   One-Way Functions and Noise

The problem with the one-way functions used with the table radon1 is that anyone who knows a person's name can look up the information about the radon levels at the person's house, the amount of smoking reported and the person's experience with cancer.

On occasion, there's no reason to add new information to a database. If that is so, it's possible to add a random number to the mix to destroy the ability to poke around the database using a person's name. If the number is forgotten after the work is done, there is no possible way to link x with $h(x)$.

Consider two databases describing some personal details about a rape victim and the location of the crime. Here are the SQL commands for creating them:

```
CREATE TABLE rape1 (nameID CHAR(32),age INT, height INT,
weight INT);
```

```
CREATE TABLE rape2 (nameID CHAR(32), stNum INT, street
CHAR(40), zip INT);
```

On occasion it may make sense for the police to link these two databases to look for correlations between the geographic information and the personal information. Both databases need the same identification string for each event.

Here's some code for initializing a Java class for adding information to the databases. At the beginning of each session, a single random number is chosen and stored in todaysRandomNum. After the session, the random number is forgotten.

```
MD5 MD5Bean=new MD5();
java.util.Random ran;
DatabaseWrapper dw=new DatabaseWrapper();
String todaysRandomNum;

public void init(){
  dw.init();
  ran=new java.util.Random();
  todaysRandomNum=""+ran.nextInt();
```

```
   initPS();
 }

PreparedStatement rape1Insert,rape2Insert;

public void initPS(){
   String q="INSERT INTO rape1 SET nameID=?,";
   q=q+"age=?,height=?,weight=?;";
   rape1Insert=dw.createPreparedStatement(q);

   q="INSERT INTO rape2 SET nameID=?,";
   q=q+"stNum=?,street=?,zip=?;";
   rape2Insert=dw.createPreparedStatement(q);
 }
```

Here are two different functions for updating the database. They can be
called at different times when different people report their results. The first,
storePersonal, can be used by a nurse after an examination. The second,
storeLocation, can be used by the officer filing a report after the event. Both
end up getting the same value of nameID because both use the same value of
todaysRandomNum.

```
public void storePersonal(String name, int age,
             int height, int weight){
 try{
 MD5Bean.clear();
 MD5Bean.Update(todaysRandomNum);
 MD5Bean.Update(name);
 rape1Insert.setString(1,MD5Bean.asHex());
 rape1Insert.setInt(2,age);
 rape1Insert.setInt(3,height);
 rape1Insert.setInt(4,weight);
 rape1Insert.executeUpdate();
 } catch (SQLException e){
   System.out.println("SQL Exception:"+e);
 }
}


public void storeLocation(String name, int num,
             String street, int zip){
 try{
 MD5Bean.clear();
 MD5Bean.Update(todaysRandomNum);
 MD5Bean.Update(name);
 rape2Insert.setString(1,MD5Bean.asHex());
 rape2Insert.setInt(2,num);
 rape2Insert.setString(3,street);
 rape2Insert.setInt(4,zip);
 rape2Insert.executeUpdate();
 } catch (SQLException e){
   System.out.println("SQL Exception:"+e);
 }
}
```

This approach clearly has some limits. If the two functions are called on
different days, then they won't generate the same value of nameID. The system

also won't work well across multiple computers unless they can synchronize their value for the random number.

Another solution is to pass the date and a secret password through a one-way function to generate the value of todaysRandomNum: $h(\text{"}swordfish/2001 - 01 - 15\text{"})$. Any computer with the password can generate the same "random" number. That may make it easier for scattered networks to create the same value of nameID, but if someone learns the password they can breach the database's translucency.

9.4   Conclusions

Quantizing the information or deleting some of the extra detail is a simple but effective way to protect sensitive data without destroying functionality. Keeping coarse detail while obscuring fine detail makes it possible for researchers to analyze the database without knowing enough to identify someone personally.

9.4.1   Lessons

- The simplest quantization algorithm is to delete unnecessary detail. When it's gone, it can't be misused.

- More sophisticated algorithms try to break the space of all possible values into subspaces called quanta. If a value lies in a quantum, then it gets the value assigned to every value in the entire quantum.

- The quanta should be small enough to provide enough detail to solve problems, but as large as possible to protect information.

- Adding noise is an effective way of blurring information while still providing enough detail. It works best in applications with a well-defined distance metric.

- Noise produced by encryption functions can be reversed effectively if the details are scrambled without destroying the information altogether.

- Encrypting the extra detail is one simple mechanism for obscuring the information without losing the information altogether.

- One-way functions can obscure the information while preserving the ability to analyze the data. The value of $h(x)$ will be the same for all values of x, but it prevents someone from learning x.

Chapter 10

Authentication

Databases need to be accurate, but they can hold only as much truth as their users provide. Ultimately, the authenticity and the integrity of the data depend upon the people who are using them. To state this in an overly simple way: if people put in good data, then the data will be good.

The real challenge is providing a tool for users to take responsibility for data. If one user vouches for the information, then others can build a layer of trust upon that responsibility.

The basic mechanism for leveraging trust in the digital realm is the *digital signature*, a term dating from the early days of public-key cryptography. The signature is a long number that can be generated only by a person holding a secret. Others can examine the number, perform some computations and, if the arithmetic works out, decide that the signature is valid.

Digital signatures bolster translucent databases in two ways. The signatures offer, first and foremost, a way to verify the information. If the databases must be secure even after attack by hackers and errant system administrators, then they need to resist efforts by people trying to insert false information. Digital signatures offer some measure of trust that the right source provided the data.

The math in this chapter is also used in Chapter 12. The digital signatures there act as tokens to retrieve records, not as promises of authenticity.

The signatures can also be used to provide security and secrecy without encryption. A translucent database can protect information without scrambling it by adding plenty of false data. Only the person with the right password can examine the digital signatures and find the right answer. The rest are left trying to separate the true from the false.

These databases filled with true and false data can be quite efficient because they can rely on well-coded tools for dealing with unencrypted data. The searching and indexing tools built into databases can remove the right information without working through a layer of encryption. After the search is done, the digital signatures can be used to choose the true information from the bad.

Both of these approaches can strengthen translucent databases by providing secure ways to tell the true from the false. The algorithms are quite powerful, but they do have limits. The promises they offer are solid, but not absolute. They are more like tools for shifting blame or shifting responsibility. They are like conduits of trust. If they shift the responsibility to the right person or computer, then the system is still valid. If they shift it the wrong direction– well, all is lost. Given proper care, though, they will provide excellent solutions that produce secure, trustworthy translucent databases with a minimal amount of overhead.

10.1   Digital Signature Taxonomy

The first digital signature algorithms emerged as an extra benefit from research into public-key algorithms. Some of the first techniques encrypted the data with one key in such a way that it could be decrypted only with a different, second key. That allowed people to publish one key and let others send messages to them by encrypting it with the public key. Only they could read it because they had the corresponding private key.

Several major algorithms also work easily in reverse. If the data was encrypted by the second, private key, then anyone with the public key could decrypt it. If the private key was really private, then the result could be produced by only the person holding it. Thus, it could act like a digital signature.

In the years that followed, the concept expanded as it entered the general vernacular. Many states and governments recognize the term *digital signature* to apply to practically any algorithm that produces something like a signature. The law tries to stay as neutral as possible so it will survive changes in technology.

The field of digital signatures is large, complicated and filled with competing standards. This chapter can't summarize all the techniques nor provide a thorough exploration of any in particular. The chapter focuses on providing the code to add digital signatures to basic SQL-compliant databases. There are better, more complicated solutions, and this chapter ignores the nuances in the interest of providing a solid explanation. Readers should consult deeper treatments if they rely heavily upon the technology to protect sensitive information.

10.1.1   One-Way Functions and Signatures

Basic one-way functions can provide simple promises of authenticity, although without the features and the flexibility of full digital signature algorithms. The basic algorithms require one secret password shared by both the signer and the verifier. This solution does not provide all of the assurance of a true digital signature because anyone who holds this password can generate the signature. The algorithms are still used often because they are more computationally efficient.

Let $h(x)$ be a one-way function and p be a password. The value of $h(p, document)$ is a result that can be computed only by someone who knows

p. This term is often called a *message authentication code*, or *MAC*, but it can also provide much of the same assurance as a proper digital signature.

Many closed networks with trusted members use these functions as digital signatures because they can be very efficient. MD5 and SHA are many times faster than the algorithms that rely on modular exponentiation for their security. One proposed micropayment scheme called Millicent relies upon a secure hash function like MD5 and dramatically lowers the cost of a central server that must process the data. [Man95]

The downside is that both the signer and the verifier must know the same value of p and thus the verifier could cheat and forge the signature. This isn't a problem in systems like Millicent because the central computer is assumed to be trustworthy. It is also not as much of a problem in some translucent databases because the value of p is not circulated widely. If it is a problem, then other algorithms can provide better, deeper security.

10.1.2 Modular Exponentiation and Signatures

There are a wide variety of digital signature schemes that rely on modular exponentiation for their security. The famous RSA algorithm created by Ron Rivest, Adi Shamir and Len Adleman uses two keys that can be swapped. If the public key does the encrypting, then only the private key can decrypt it. A digital signature emerges when the private key does the encrypting. Then anyone with the public key can test the truth.

Diffie-Hellman Key exchange is used in Section 4.2 to hide data.

In the interest of completeness and variety, this chapter describes a different type of digital signature sometimes called a *Diffie-Hellman Signature*, a term based on the deepest roots of its heritage. Whitfield Diffie and Martin Hellman developed a way for two people to agree upon a key in the presence of eavesdroppers. Many others followed in their wake and used similar techniques to create digital signatures. This approach descends from all of them.

This algorithm depends upon the intractable nature of the discrete log problem. The private key is a number, x, that may be found by applying a one-way function to some password: $h(password)$. The public key is the combination of a prime number, p; a number smaller than the prime, g; and the result $g^x \bmod p$. If the discrete log problem is truly hard, there should be no way for someone to take the information in the public key and compute x, the private key.

The day is never so dark, nor the night even, but that the laws at least of light still prevail, and so may make it light in our minds if they are open to the truth.
*–**Henry David Thoreau** Letter, Dec. 19, 1854, to Harrison Blake*

A digital signature is constructed with this information by the following steps:

1. The data to be signed is passed through a one-way function, which produces a value, $c = h(document)$, known as the *challenge* by some.

2. The signer creates a random value, w, often called a *witness*. The signer computes $g^w \bmod p$.

3. The signer computes $r = cx + w$ and discards w. Only the signer should be able to compute this number because only the signer knows w and

x.

4. The signer computes $g^r \bmod p$.

5. The signature consists of r and $g^w \bmod p$.

These three values made up of the digital signature. Anyone who wants to test these can use this algorithm:

1. The verifier begins with $g^x \bmod p$, the public key.

2. The verifier computes the one-way function applied to the document: $c = h(document)$.

3. The verifier computes $(g^x \bmod p)^{-c} \, mod \, p = g^{-cx} \bmod p$.

4. The verifier takes the digital signature and computes $g^r \bmod p$.

5. Then the verifier multiplies $(g^r \bmod p)$ by $g^{-cx} \bmod p$ to get

$$g^r g^{-cx} = g^{cx+w} g^{-cx} = g^w \bmod p.$$

If that matches the value of $g^w \bmod p$ given in the signature, then it is consistent. The signature is said to be valid.

Is this secure? Could it be produced by only someone who knows the secret value of x? Anyone can compute $g^r \bmod p$ by raising $g^x \bmod p$ to the power of c and then multiplying it by $g^w \bmod p$. But the verifier won't be using that value. The verifier will be starting with r. Notice that r does not reveal x because w has scrambled it. The signature verifier does not have access to w itself, just $g^w \bmod p$. So the signature verifier can't use the information to find x.

Many newer digital signature algorithms use variations that may offer more security. The Secure Hash Algorithm is a complement to the official U.S. government Digital Signature Algorithm, which is a more sophisticated version of the algorithm presented here.

10.2 Adding Digital Signatures to SQL Databases

Adding a digital signature is as simple as adding the extra fields to hold the information. Each row can hold extra fields that verify the information in the official fields.

The biggest challenge is keeping the data in the right format to ensure that the signatures compute correctly. Digital signature algorithms are very unforgiving. Any slight change can produce results that don't match at all. Unfortunately, digital signatures can't report that a certain row is close. It's either exactly correct or completely off.

10.2.1 A Hash-based Signature

The baby sitter example in Chapter 5 is as good a place to begin as any. Here's the SQL command creating another version of the database:

```
CREATE TABLE babysitter3 (idHash CHAR(32), name BLOB,
description TINYTEXT, free TINYINT, eventType TINYINT,
eventStart DATETIME, eventEnd DATETIME, checkHash CHAR(32));
```

This is the same as `babysitter2` except it comes with an extra column, `checkHash`, that will contain a digital signature of the rest of the information.

Imagine that an attacker or a malicious system administrator decides to insert fake data to thwart the money-earning potential of one baby sitter. That system administrator may not know the baby sitter's password, but that doesn't stop the creation of fake entries. The attacker can grab likely `idHash` values and create entirely new entries with the information. Maybe some information in the `description` column gives away the baby sitter's schedule. Perhaps it is busy at set times. The attacker may not be able to pick out the exact value of `idHash`, but even several hundred likely candidates aren't a challenge. The attacker can keep a baby sitter from getting business by inserting fake records that claim the sitter is forever busy on Friday and Saturday nights.

This version uses the `PreparedStatement` feature of the JDBC:

```
PreparedStatement babysitter3Insert;
public void initbabysitter3(){
  String q="INSERT INTO babysitter3 SET ";
  q=q+"idHash=?,name=?,description=?,";
  q=q+"free=?,eventType=?,eventStart=?,";
  q=q+"eventEnd=?,checkHash=?;";
  babysitter3Insert=dw.createPreparedStatement(q);
}
```

The `babysitter3Insert` is precomputed. The question marks are replaced by particular values using statements tuned for each data type.

The digital signature is computed in Java using the `MD5Bean`. The essential data elements from the entry are added to the signature using the `Update` method. The information is passed into the `Update` method as a `String`. It is important that this format is preserved because it the digital signature will not work because the format is not exact.

Here's the code:

```
public void insertWithCheck(String sitterName,
  String sitterPassword,
  String description,
  int freeOrBusy,
  int eventType,
  Date eventStart,
  Date eventEnd){

MD5Bean.clear();
MD5Bean.Update(sitterName);
MD5Bean.Update(sitterPassword);
```

```
// extract the idHash from this calculation.
 String idHash=MD5Bean.asHex();

MD5Bean.Update(description);
MD5Bean.Update(""+freeOrBusy+eventType);
System.out.println("hashing:"+eventStart+eventEnd);
MD5Bean.Update(eventStart.toString()+eventEnd.toString());
String hash=MD5Bean.asHex();

try{
  babysitter3Insert.setString(1,idHash);

  String messagePassword=generatePrivatePassword(sitterName,sitterPassword);
  String encodedName=encode(sitterName,messagePassword);
  babysitter3Insert.setString(2,encodedName);// unencrypted
  babysitter3Insert.setString(3,description);
  babysitter3Insert.setInt(4,freeOrBusy);
  babysitter3Insert.setInt(5,eventType);
  babysitter3Insert.setTimestamp(6,new Timestamp(eventStart.getTime()));
  babysitter3Insert.setTimestamp(7,new Timestamp(eventEnd.getTime()));
  babysitter3Insert.setString(8,hash);

  //  babysitter3Insert.executeUpdate();
} catch (Exception e){
  System.out.println("Problems with:"+e);
}

}
```

Notice that the encrypted field `name` is not included in the signature. That is because the `sitterName` variable is the first one to be pushed into the `MD5Bean`. It is already part of the signature. The encrypted version could also be included for completeness, but it would be cumbersome here.

Notice also the typecasting done to insert the two Java `Date` values, `eventStart` and `eventEnd`. The standard SQL `Timestamp` value includes a place for nanoseconds. The Java `Date` object doesn't. So the JDBC includes an extra object, `Timestamp`, that is a superset of `Date`. It is important to keep these two straight because the `toString` functions are not the same. The Java `Date` has a complicated, multilanguage feature that can easily convert between the date notations used in different countries. The `Timestamp` comes with the SQL's standard way of rendering a date. If these aren't used consistently, then the signature will be off.

Here's some code for inserting a test value:

```
public void constructSomeDates(){
  initbabysitter3();
  String sitter="Mary B. Goode";
  String password="swordfish";
  Calendar timer=Calendar.getInstance();
  timer.clear();
  timer.set(2002,Calendar.JANUARY,3,14,0);
  Date startTime=timer.getTime();

  timer.clear();
  timer.set(2002,Calendar.JANUARY,3,20,0);
```

```
Date endTime=timer.getTime();

insertWithCheck(sitter,password,"No practice.",1,1,startTime,endTime);
}
```

The previous examples did not use the Java Date objects to hold the times because the times did not have to be exactly the same before and after they were stored and recovered from the database. The Java Date objects act as canonical values which always display the dates in the same way. That may be a bit more cumbersome that typing in your own string, but it guarantees that the signature will be the same.

Well, the promise is not perfect. The flexibility of Java means that the dates will be displayed differently in the U.S. and in other countries. If you're going to use that feature, you must be sure that everyone who accesses the database uses the same Locale to format the dates. Sigh.

Executing that function leaves the database looking like this:

Column	Value
idHash	8393f37be25ccdf593cf641755272854
name	8bkfka89zx09j3l2jljjl23
description	No practice.
free	1
eventType	1
eventStart	01-03 14:00:00
eventEnd	01-03 20:00:00
checkHash	30e8d8dbfd3805089746a6183a9730dc

The checkHash field is the digital signature. It depends upon the sitterName, sitterPassword, freeOrBusy, eventType, eventStart and eventEnd fields. It can be generated only by someone who knows the sitterName and sitterPassword values. Any random Joe with access to the database can't concoct entries that make sense. The idHash and the data in the row must be consistent, thanks to the checkHash field.

Here's some Java code for looking up a baby sitter and checking the consistency of the digital signature.

```
public void lookupWithCheck(String sitterName,
  String sitterPassword){

  MD5Bean.clear();
  MD5Bean.Update(sitterName);
  MD5Bean.Update(sitterPassword);
// extract the idHash from this calculation.
  String idHash=MD5Bean.asHex();
  try{
    String qu="SELECT * FROM babysitter3 WHERE idHash='";
    qu+=idHash+"';");
    ResultSet rs=dw.executeQuery(qu);
    rs.next();
```

```
int freeOrBusy=rs.getInt("free");
int eventType=rs.getInt("eventType");
String description=rs.getString("description");
Date startEvent=new Date(rs.getTimestamp("eventStart").getTime());
Date endEvent=new Date(rs.getTimestamp("eventEnd").getTime());
String checkHash=rs.getString("checkHash");

// Now compute the checkhash ourselves.
MD5Bean.Update(description);
 MD5Bean.Update(""+freeOrBusy+eventType);
System.out.println("hashing:"+startEvent+endEvent);

MD5Bean.Update(startEvent.toString()+endEvent);
String hash=MD5Bean.asHex();

if (!hash.equals(checkHash)){
  System.out.println("There's an error.");
} else {
  System.out.println("Found correct data.");
}
} catch (Exception e){
  System.out.println("Problem with:"+e);
}
}
```

Notice that the values for startEvent and endEvent go through an elaborate typecasting. The Timestamp object begets a new Date object, using the universal long integer representation of the date. That is because the Timestamp is a descendant of Date, but one that comes with a different toString method. In my original version of the code, I didn't do this and ended up with a signature that could not be verified.

10.2.2 Signatures Using Exponentiation

The digital signatures in Section 10.2.1 are useful against some attackers, but not all. Anyone who knows a baby sitter's name and password can fill in all the required fields and compute the value of the MD5 hash. That may block an odd system administrator or hacker, but it won't stop someone who knows the basic password. In some of the earlier examples in Chapter 5, the password is given to any acceptable parent.

Here's another example using the pubkeys database from Chapter 4. The public keys in that table were used to encrypt messages intended for particular recipients. In this example, they are used to verify messages from people using a digital signature.

Imagine that there's a central database containing information about upcoming rock shows. Fans carefully watch it, waiting to see a show with their favorite artists. Clearly, access to this database can be misused to create a denial-of-service attack on anyone. All you need to do is post the target's phone number and announce that it is the one source for tickets for a very popular teen band and kids will stay up all night calling that number. Digital signatures can prevent that problem.

The public key in pubkeys consists of g,p and g^x mod p. The value of x is the private key found from putting the passphrase through a one-way function. Here's the SQL command creating the rockshows table:

```
CREATE TABLE rockshows (showinfo TEXT, poster TINYTEXT, geew
TINYTEXT, r TINYTEXT, c TINYTEXT, geer TINYTEXT);
```

The message announcing the show is placed in the column showinfo. The person responsible for the message is stored in poster. This name should match exactly a name in the name column of the pubkeys database so anyone can recover the right public key.

The signature is placed in the other columns:

Value	column
g^w mod p	geew
g^r mod p	geer
r	r
c	c

The values c and g^r mod p are redundant. They are not needed, but I included them for illustration. They make debugging easier.

Here's a function that posts a message in the rockshows database with these steps:

1. Looks up the public key in pubkeys.

2. Constructs the private key by hashing the passphrase with the MD5Bean.

3. Calculates $c = h(message)$ with MD5Bean.

4. Creates a random value, w, to act as a witness.

5. Computes g^w mod p, $r = cx + w$ and g^r mod p.

6. Inserts them into the database. g^r mod p is not needed to check the signature.

```
public void signMessage(String signer,
             String passphrase,
             String message){
  String findQuery="SELECT * FROM pubkeys WHERE name='"+signer+"';";
  try{
    ResultSet rs=dw.executeQuery(findQuery);
    rs.next(); // get the first match of public key.

    String gee=rs.getString("gee");
    String pea=rs.getString("pea");
    String geex=rs.getString("geex");

    BigInteger gx=new BigInteger(geex);
    BigInteger p=new BigInteger(pea);
```

```
      BigInteger g=new BigInteger(gee);


      // build private key.

      MD5Bean.clear();
      MD5Bean.Update("Translucent Databases rock.");
      MD5Bean.Update(passphrase);
      byte[] hashedPass=MD5Bean.Final();
      BigInteger x=new BigInteger(hashedPass);

      // hash message.

      MD5Bean.clear();
      MD5Bean.Update("Start a signature here.");
      MD5Bean.Update(message);
      byte[] hashedMessage=MD5Bean.Final();
      BigInteger c=new BigInteger(hashedMessage);


      BigInteger w=new BigInteger(760,5,new Random());
      BigInteger gw=g.modPow(w,p);

      BigInteger r=w.add(c.multiply(x));
      BigInteger gr=g.modPow(r,p);


      StringBuffer a=new StringBuffer();
      a.append("INSERT into rockshows SET ");
      a.append(" showinfo='"+message+"', ");
      a.append(" poster='"+signer+"', ");
      a.append(" geew='"+gw.toString()+"', ");
      a.append(" r='"+r.toString()+"', ");
      a.append(" c='"+c.toString()+"', ");
      a.append(" geer='"+gr.toString()+"' ");
      a.append(";");
      dw.executeUpdate(a.toString());

  } catch (Exception e){
     System.out.println("Problems with:"+e);
  }
}
```

Executing signMessage with the parameters of "H. Jones", "tomatoes"
and "Rockpile One Night Only At the Paladium. Call 212-555-1234
for tickets" produces the SQL line:

```
INSERT into rockshows SET showinfo='Rockpile One Night Only
At the Paladium.  Call 212-555-1234 for tickets', poster='H.
Jones', geew='34021976791210932187726278953996494759447
0164332893957776559728  7...',
r='30582755744144731310017472240093916175654684351109  1320  1-
7382441436830...',
c='1273040471167261313217930533182110985  17',
geer='48492043005217337145846373588631994569285111366  1096-
```

30611771988088...'
;

The result is checked with the Java method `retrieveMessageAndCheck`, which uses these steps to ensure that only valid messages are recovered:

1. Recover the public key from `pubkeys`.

2. Convert the public key into `BigIntegers`.

3. Recover the first message from `poster` in `rockshows`.

4. Convert the signature into `BigIntegers`.

5. Compute $c_2 = h(message)$. Ideally, that should match c. This must be recomputed to verify that no one changed the value of `message` in the database. For this reason, there's no real purpose in storing or recovering c from `rockshows`.

6. Compute $(g^x \bmod p)^{c_2} \times g^w \bmod p$. This relies upon the value of $g^x \bmod p$ recovered from the `pubkeys` table.

7. Computes $g^r \bmod p$ using r from `rockshows`.

8. Compares the three different values.

```
public void retrieveMessageAndCheck(String poster){
   String findQuery="SELECT * FROM pubkeys WHERE name='"+poster+"';";
   try{
     ResultSet rs=dw.executeQuery(findQuery);
     rs.next(); // get the first match of public key.

     String gee=rs.getString("gee");
     String pea=rs.getString("pea");
     String geex=rs.getString("geex");

     BigInteger gx=new BigInteger(geex);
     BigInteger p=new BigInteger(pea);
     BigInteger g=new BigInteger(gee);

     // recover message.
     String query2="SELECT * FROM rockshows WHERE poster='"+poster+"';";
     ResultSet rs2=dw.executeQuery(query2);
     rs2.next(); // do the first one only.

     BigInteger geew=new BigInteger(rs2.getString("geew"));
     BigInteger c=new BigInteger(rs2.getString("c"));
     BigInteger r=new BigInteger(rs2.getString("r"));
     BigInteger geer=new BigInteger(rs2.getString("geer"));

     // check the hash.
     String message=rs2.getString("showinfo");
     MD5Bean.clear();
     MD5Bean.Update("Start a signature here.");
     MD5Bean.Update(message);
```

```
byte[] hashedMessage=MD5Bean.Final();
BigInteger c2=new BigInteger(hashedMessage);

BigInteger geer2=(gx.modPow(c2,p)).multiply(geew).mod(p);
BigInteger geer3=g.modPow(r,p);


if ((geer.equals(geer2) && (geer2.equals(geer3))){
  System.out.println("Message from "+poster+":"+message);
} else {
  System.out.println("Forgery detected:"+message);
}


} catch (Exception e){
  System.out.println("Problems with:"+e);
}
}
```

If this is executed using the data stored before, the values match and the message is validated. Incorrect data will trigger a flag signaling a forgery.

The approach in this example is not the most efficient solution. This book aims to illustrate the principles of translucent databases, not provide the best and most efficient tools for producing digital signatures. This example was chosen because it uses the same public keys from pubkeys in Chapter 4. A better solution may be to use an algorithm optimized for the digital signature, like the Digital Signature Standard.

This translucent database has several advantages over the signatures used in Section 10.2.1. The person verifying the signature does not need to know the key ("tomatoes") that generates the signature. That person just needs access to pubkeys.

10.3   Fake Information

Mixing in incorrect or spurious information is one of the time-honored techniques for disrupting eavesdroppers. Most of the techniques in this book scramble information to block hackers, but there's no reason why fake information can't serve the same purpose. If the person poking around the inside of the database can't tell which rows are real and which are fake, then there's little information being revealed. It's not exactly the same as no information, but it's not bad.

The efficiency of this solution is not high. If the real information is to be indistinguishable from the fake, then all possible fakes should be possible. In the most extreme sense, if there are i bits of real data, then there should be $2^i - 1$ entries containing all possible combinations of fake bits. That may be possible if $i = 1$ or perhaps $i = 2$, but it quickly grows impossible.

Most applications don't need this theoretical security. A database containing the travel plans for executives may list three destinations and several different routes to each destination. A kidnapper would not be able to focus on just one route, and that might be enough to disrupt a crime. Of course, the real information is still mixed into the database. The kidnapper may be able to use other information to reduce the possibilities and maybe settle on the one true route. Creating efficient databases filled with a limited number of decoys is more of an art than a science.

This technique may not be very space-efficient, but it can save computer cycles. Scrambling the route information may block eavesdroppers, but it also makes searching and sorting difficult if not impossible. Imagine that there is one column in the departure time. If that is encrypted or hashed, there's no easy way to search this column for trips leaving tomorrow without unscrambling every item. If the one-way functions or the encryption is good, then there won't be any correlation between the scrambled and the unscrambled version.

Ron Rivest suggested using fake information to produce encryption with pure authentication algorithms. His work dated from a time when some parts of the U.S. government viewed encryption as dangerous but authentication as good.[Riv98]

A database filled with fake trip information, however, can store this departure time in the clear. A search of the database for this column is easy to do with the built-in search and index features. The results will still contain a number of fakes, but those can be weeded out after the fact. If the database is large and filled with the travel plans of many executives, then this solution could be more efficient. Not unscrambling each departure time is a big saving.

10.3.1 An Appointment System

Here's an appointment system built out of Java and SQL. The database contains one table, appointments1, which holds real and fake appointments. The Java code calculates digital signatures and inserts appointments with them. Real appointments get real signatures, and fake appointments get bad ones.

The database is created with this SQL code:

```
CREATE TABLE appointments1 (name TINYTEXT, meetingWith
TINYTEXT, description TEXT,appStart DATETIME, appEnd
DATETIME, hashCode CHAR(32));
```

The name of the person holding the appointment is stored in name, the name of the other half of the appointment is in meetingWith, and the location and other details end up in description. The times are stored in appStart and appEnd. The name is not protected with a one-way function in this example because the extra counterfeit entries perform the same purpose.

Each person gets a passcode that must be entered correctly to add an appointment or check to see whether the appointment is real. The Java code doesn't use any of the precautions suggested in Section 3.2 to prevent typographic errors, but it could. The digital signature here is created by computing the MD5 hash of the names, the location, and the time of the appointment. You can't distinguish between the real and the fake entries without the correct value of passcode.

10.3.2   Adding Entries With Signatures

Here is some basic code executed when the Java code begins. It starts the random number generator and creates two `PreparedStatements`, used to add new entries and retrieve old ones from the `appointments1` table.

```
MD5 MD5Bean=new MD5();
java.util.Random ran;
DatabaseWrapper dw=new DatabaseWrapper();
Calendar timeMachine1,timeMachine2;

public void init(){
  dw.init();
  ran=new java.util.Random();
  initAppointments1();
  timeMachine1 = Calendar.getInstance();
  timeMachine2 = Calendar.getInstance();
}


PreparedStatement appInsert,lookup;

public void initAppointments1(){
  String q="INSERT INTO appointments1 SET ";
  q=q+"name=?,meetingWith=?,description=?,";
  q=q+"appStart=?,appEnd=?,hashcode=?;";
  appInsert=dw.createPreparedStatement(q);

  q="SELECT * FROM appointments1 WHERE ";
  q=q+"name=? AND appStart<=? AND appEnd>=?;";
  lookup=dw.createPreparedStatement(q);
}
```

Here's the basic code for inserting a new entry into the table. The signature is computed by hashing the `name`, `meetingWith`, and `location` variables together with the `String` versions of the `java.util.Dates`. The hash function is made unique by starting with the `passcode` and the phrase "An Ordered Calendar Means an Ordered Life." Anyone who wants to test the signatures must have both. The extra phrase is more like a `passcode` shared between developers. Someone reverse-engineering the process must know it. No one can work from observation.

If this is a fake signature (the `realEntry` is `false`), then an integer produced by the `Random` number generator is mixed into the hash function. In either case, the results are jammed into the `appInsert` `PreparedStatement` and fed to the database.

```
public void insertAppointment(String name,
                String passcode,
                String meetingWith,
                String location,
                java.util.Date start,
                java.util.Date end,
```

```
                        boolean realEntry){
  // compute hash digital signature
  MD5Bean.clear();
  if (!realEntry){
    MD5Bean.Update(ran.nextInt());
  } else {
      MD5Bean.Update("An Ordered Calendar means an Ordered Life.");
      MD5Bean.Update(passcode);// do the password first.
      MD5Bean.Update(name);
      MD5Bean.Update(meetingWith);
      MD5Bean.Update(location);
      MD5Bean.Update(start.toString());
      MD5Bean.Update(end.toString());
  }
  String hashcode=MD5Bean.asHex();

  // Store this.
  try{
    appInsert.setString(1,name);
    appInsert.setString(2,meetingWith);
    appInsert.setString(3,location);
    appInsert.setTimestamp(4,new java.sql.Timestamp(start.getTime()));
    appInsert.setTimestamp(5,new java.sql.Timestamp(end.getTime()));
    appInsert.setString(6,hashcode);

    appInsert.executeUpdate();
  } catch (SQLException e){
    System.out.println("SQLException:"+e);
  }
}
```

10.3.3 Adding Fake Entries

Creating fake entries is an art with no guarantees. Unless you add a large number of fakes, the odds of discovering the real ones remain significant. This example tries to minimize the danger by probing the database and finding similar appointments.

This code fetches all the meetings held by a person and pulls out the names of the other person at the meeting. The location is also grabbed to keep things consistent. It doesn't do much good to obscure a meeting with the president at 1600 Pennsylvania Avenue with other meetings at the conference room down the hall.

```
public Vector getOtherMeetings(String name){
// returns a list of names that name meets with.
  Vector ans=new Vector();
  try{
  String q="SELECT meetingWith,description FROM appointments1 WHERE name='";
  q+=name+"';";
  ResultSet rs=dw.executeQuery(q);
  while (rs.next()){
      ans.addElement(rs.getString(1));
      ans.addElement(rs.getString(2));
  }
```

```
  } catch (SQLException e){
    System.out.println("SQLException:"+e);
  }
  return ans;
}
```

This code could be more elaborate. The code grabs the names of all people in the database. If that includes old records, it will grab the names of people who aren't at the firm any longer. A sleuth may be able to use insights like that to winnow out the fakes.

The function `addAppointment` adds one real appointment before obscuring it with a random number of fake appointments, using these steps:

1. The real appoinment is inserted, using `insertAppointment` with `realEntry` set to `true`.

2. A collection of old appointments is assembled, using `getOtherMeetings`.

3. The number of fake meetings is chosen, using two random numbers for `before` and `howMany`. The number of fake entries before the current real appointment is governed by the size of `before`. The number that fall after is set by `howMany`.

4. The code uses the Java `Calendar` objects to change the dates. They make it easy to add or subtract an arbitrary number of minutes with the `add(Calendar.MINUTE,amount)` command. The object handles the carry over that can change hours and days.

5. The code adds new appointments in increments of 30 minutes at a time. This is an arbitrary number which might be better changed to 15 or 10.

6. The fake appointments choose a random person and location to go with the time.

7. The fake appointments are stored, using `insertAppointment`.

```
public void addAppointment(String name,
                String passcode,
                String meetingWith,
                String location,
                java.util.Date start,
                java.util.Date end){
// Insert real one.
insertAppointment(name,passcode,meetingWith,location,start,end,true);

//Insert fake times.
timeMachine1.setTime(start);
timeMachine2.setTime(end);

Vector otherPeople=getOtherMeetings(name);
int ii=ran.nextInt();
```

```
    int before=Math.abs(ii % 5);
    ii=ran.nextInt();
    int howMany=Math.abs(ii % 5);
    int with;

    // roll back
    timeMachine1.add(Calendar.MINUTE,-before * 30);
    timeMachine2.add(Calendar.MINUTE,-before *30);
    for (int i=0;i<before;i++){
        // select random guy;
        with=Math.abs(ran.nextInt() % otherPeople.size());
        if (1== (with % 2)) with--; // keep it even.

        insertAppointment(name,passcode,(String) otherPeople.elementAt(with),
                (String) otherPeople.elementAt(with+1),
                timeMachine1.getTime(),timeMachine2.getTime(),false);
        timeMachine1.add(Calendar.MINUTE,30);
        timeMachine2.add(Calendar.MINUTE,30);
    }
        timeMachine1.add(Calendar.MINUTE,30);
        timeMachine2.add(Calendar.MINUTE,30);
            // don't add the same time twice.

    for (int i=0;i<howMany;i++){
        // select random guy;
        with=Math.abs(ran.nextInt() % otherPeople.size());
        if (1== (with % 2)) with--; // keep it even.

        insertAppointment(name,passcode,(String) otherPeople.elementAt(with),
                (String) otherPeople.elementAt(with+1),
                timeMachine1.getTime(),timeMachine2.getTime(),false);
        timeMachine1.add(Calendar.MINUTE,30);
        timeMachine2.add(Calendar.MINUTE,30);
    }
}
```

There are probably many different ways that this code could be written. Adding several fake appointments before and after the real appointment may add distraction. The solution, though, may be statistically imperfect because the real appointment is likely to be near the center of a block of appointments. If many appointments are on the calendar, then they will all blend together.

Another solution is to add the fake appointments for the same time. That removes the chance an attacker will use the sequence to find the real appointment, but it does mean that an attacker will be able to find the correct time.

More robust solutions call for more and more decoys, and that can get more expensive. The number of decoys is chosen for each database, depending on the needs for efficiency. Some insight may be gained by using information theory to model the entropy of the appointment streams, but that is beyond the scope of this book.

Here's an example of the database with three real entries:

name	meetingWith	description	appStart	appEnd	hashCode
H. Jones	Margo Beatnik	RM M56	03-02 12:30	03-02 02:30	5dd5a...
H. Jones	Robert Bialy	M776	03-03 01:00	03-03 02:30	27bbb...
H. Jones	Candace O'Malley	K33	03-02 09:00	03-02 10:30	8daa3...

Here's the database after using `addAppointment` to add one real and five fake entries:

name	meetingWith	description	appStart	appEnd	hashCode
H. Jones	Margo Beatnik	RM M56	03-02 12:30	03-02 02:30	5dd5a...
H. Jones	Robert Bialy	M776	03-03 01:00	03-03 02:30	27bbb...
H. Jones	Candace O'Malley	K33	03-02 09:00	03-02 10:30	8daa3...
H. Jones	Caroline O'Shea	M36	03-04 02:30	03-04 06:00	be83f...
H. Jones	Margo Beatnik	RM M56	03-04 02:00	03-04 05:30	d6515...
H. Jones	Robert Bialy	M776	03-04 00:30	03-04 04:00	2b3e5...
H. Jones	Margo Beatnik	RM M56	03-04 01:00	03-04 04:30	c4504...
H. Jones	Caroline O'Shea	M36	03-04 01:30	03-04 05:00	afd90...
H. Jones	Caroline O'Shea	M36	03-04 01:00	03-04 04:30	d5a07...

10.3.4   Finding the Results

This mechanism shines when it is time to search the database. The information is all left in the clear so optimal algorithms for extracting the right information can be used without concern for the effects of encryption and security.

This code uses the `lookup` PreparedStatement to find all the results that intersect with a particular time. That is with an `appStart` which comes before the moment and an `appEnd` value, which comes after. These are the appointments that may be real enough to prevent someone from scheduling a new appointment.

The code obviously recovers many fakes. If the code above is used, there should be about five to six fakes for every real response. While this can be cumbersome, it can be much simpler than decoding the entire column.

The code tests the signatures by using the `passcode` provided to it. The ones that match come spitting out. There should be only one if the database is not filled with someone double-booking appointments.

```
public void checkAppointments(String name,String passcode,
                              java.util.Date time){
 try{
  lookup.setString(1,name);
  java.sql.Timestamp ts=new java.sql.Timestamp(time.getTime());
  lookup.setTimestamp(2,ts);
  lookup.setTimestamp(3,ts);

  ResultSet rs=lookup.executeQuery();

  String meetingWith,location;
  java.util.Date start,end;
  String storedHash,foundHash;
  while (rs.next()){
    meetingWith=rs.getString("meetingWith");
    location=rs.getString("description");
    start=new java.util.Date(rs.getTimestamp("appStart").getTime());
    end=new java.util.Date(rs.getTimestamp("appEnd").getTime());
    storedHash=rs.getString("hashCode");

    // Check it
    MD5Bean.clear();
```

```
    MD5Bean.Update("An Ordered Calendar means an Ordered Life.");
    MD5Bean.Update(passcode);// do the password first.
    MD5Bean.Update(name);
    MD5Bean.Update(meetingWith);
    MD5Bean.Update(location);
    MD5Bean.Update(start.toString());
    MD5Bean.Update(end.toString());
    foundHash=MD5Bean.asHex();
    if (foundHash.equals(storedHash)){
      System.out.println("Found appointment:"+name+" with "+meetingWith);
      System.out.println("Starting:"+start+" Ending:"+end);
      System.out.println("Location:"+location);
    }
  }
} catch (SQLException e){
  System.out.println("SQLException:"+e);
}
```

10.3.5 Modifications

This is a very basic solution. The table in the database can be extended by using the tricks from Chapter 5, where the more complicated examples for the baby sitter solve the same basic problem. This appointment system could also use a separate table to control access to the data itself. This table could give others access to the schedule of people by giving them the password that would allow them to check the signature.

Another solution is to use public-key signatures, like the ones described in Section 10.2.2. These public keys could be distributed to those with a need to distinguish between the real and the fake without giving them the ability to create real signatures. Of course, if the keys circulate too freely, the security of the database can be compromised. A more elaborate example would use public keys to verify the data and would control access to these keys with a secondary table, like the one used to control access to baby sitter schedules in Chapter 5.

An interesting question is whether the techniques in Chapter 5 or the techniques in this chapter are better. Leaving the information in the clear allows the database engine to work faster, but pushing the information through a one-way function is more secure.

10.4   Conclusions

The authenticity of the data is a crucial problem for any database manager. This chapter described two basic techniques for generating signatures as well as a way to exploit the techniques. Some databases just use the digital signatures to block interlopers. Others add fake data to thwart casual browsers.

10.4.1 Lessons

- Digital signatures are extra bits that can test whether data is unchanged. That is, a person creates a digital signature by looking at the data and affixing some extra numbers. If the numbers and the equations work out correctly, then the signatures are still valid.

- Digital signatures can be much better than paper signatures because any small change in the data will break them. The systems are very fragile.

- If the private key is compromised, however, digital signatures become very easy to forge.

- The simplest digital signatures use one-way functions and a password: $h(password, data)$. These are often called Message Authentication Codes. They are usually fast because an efficient hash function like MD5 or SHA can be used. The same password must be present to test the signature, a dangerous feature that gives the person verifying a signature the ability to create new ones.

- Public-key encryption algorithms use two keys to generate digital signatures. The public one is available to anyone to test the signature, but only its private cousin can create them.

- Adding fake messages to a database and then using digital signatures is one way to leave information unscrambled while obscuring it.

Chapter 11

Accounting

Some one-way functions completely scramble information. Hash functions like MD5 or SHA produce a number that is close to random. There's no way to use your knowledge about $MD5(x)$ and $MD5(y)$ to learn anything about x and y. The one-way function is completely opaque to any query except testing equality.

Other one-way functions have some mathematical properties that permit basic arithmetic without removing the translucent veil of secrecy. If $h(x) = g^x \bmod p$, then you can learn a fair amount about x and y from studying $h(x)$ and $h(y)$. You will not learn the values of x and y, but you can check and confirm some basic arithmetic.

Consider these facts:

- $(g^x \bmod p)(g^y \bmod p) \bmod p = g^{x+y} \bmod p$.

- $(g^x \bmod p)^c \bmod p = g^{cx} \bmod p$.

- $\frac{g^x \bmod p}{g^y \bmod p} \bmod p = g^{x-y} \bmod p$.

These mean that you can do basic accounting with numbers hidden by one-way functions using exponentiation modulo a prime number. Instead of adding two values, you multiply them modulo the prime. Instead of multiplying two numbers, you raise one to a power modulo a prime.

These three operations are all computationally feasible, although they are far from efficient when compared with doing the work with ordinary, unscrambled values. Addition is one of the fastest operations on a general CPU. Multiplying two values modulo a prime is feasible, but much more computationally demanding especially when the computations are done modulo a relatively long prime number. Unfortunately, the discrete log problem is hard enough to be daunting only when p has hundreds, if not thousands, of digits.

Some operations are truly not feasible, and this creates limits. There's no known way to take $g^x \bmod p$ and find x. This means that some computations can't really be done. You may be able to add x and y by multiplying $g^x \bmod p$

and $g^y \bmod p$ to get $g^{x+y} \bmod p$, but you can't find out the answer because there's no way to take $g^{x+y} \bmod p$ and find $x + y$.

That can lead to some annoying difficulties. Debugging is next to impossible. A checkbook register kept with this mechanism is either going to add up correctly or fail miserably. There's no way to add everything up and determine that the discrepancy is only four cents.

There can be loopholes if the numbers are small enough. There may be no general way to take $g^x \bmod p$ and find x, but if all the values are small enough, it is possible to use some brute force. It is practical to calculate $g^2 \bmod p, g^3 \bmod p, g^4 \bmod p \ldots$. Inverting $g^x \bmod p$ can be done by iterating through a range of values of i and stopping when $g^i = g^x \bmod p$.

That can either be an opportunity or a security gap. If most numbers are big enough to come from a set too large for a brute-force search, then this technique provides an opportunity for debugging when the set can be narrowed. It may not be feasible to invert all the values of $g^x \bmod p$ on the balance sheet of a corporation with billions and billions of dollars, but possible to unmask errors of less than \$100.

If brute-force attacks are a danger, the size of the potential set can be increased dramatically by adding fake digits. If x normally comes from values between 0 and 999, then the set can be enlarged by adding a random value multiplied by $10,000$ to x. So $x = 594$ could become 14124214123531520594 and $y = 15$ could become $y = 512512351235123410015$. The last four digits of $x + y$ are still consistent, but it is practically impossible to use brute force to uncover the values of x, y or $x + y$.

The arithmetic that can and can't be done in this system can be hard to understand. On one hand, you can easily add up two columns of numbers and ensure that they produce the same total, a technique that's useful in bookkeeping. On the other, you can't do much with the information except check to confirm that they add up to the same value. Small discrepaencies can be easy to find, but many will want to trade away this feature for a useful defense against brute-force attack.

11.1   Sales Force Accounting

Imagine you have a salesforce who receive a significant part of their salaries from commissions. The database keeping track of their commissions clearly contains sensitive information. Some businesses may actually want to publicize who is bringing in big numbers as an incentive, while others may try to keep the information quiet. In any case, the sales force would have a good incentive to tamper with the database to increase their salaries.

Here's a basic example that keeps two tables in the database and checks to establish they're consistent. One holds the names of the salespeople and the commission they have earned. The other keeps track of the sales for each product line.

```
CREATE TABLE commission (name CHAR(40), totalCommission
TEXT);

CREATE TABLE products (productLine CHAR(40), totalSales
TEXT);
```

The names of the salespeople and the itmes in the product line are left in the clear. The amounts of sales are stored in long text strings showing very long integers. A better solution may be to use BLOBs, or binary representations, to save space and increase speed. This solution, while a bit inefficient, makes some debugging easier.

In this case, the sales force is organized geographically so any salesperson can sell any product. At the end of the day, week, month, quarter or year, though, the total sales of products should be consistent with the commissions paid. Each salesperson receives a commission of 10 percent, a number that is easy to compute and check in this example.

When a new sale is recorded, the result is added to both the salesperson's table and the product line database. Unfortunately, this scheme does place some limitations on precision. Rounding-off errors can prove fatal because small inconsistencies do not balance out. For that reason, this example assumes that all sales are priced in increments of $10 so that commissions will always be in whole dollars. There is no need to record cents.

The arithmetic is not difficult. Here are the steps taken to add x to the record of a salesperson:

1. The old value, $g^y \bmod p$, is recovered.

2. $g^x \bmod p$ is computed.

3. x is added by computing $(g^x \bmod p)(g^y \bmod p) \bmod p = g^{x+y} \bmod p$.

4. This result is stored in the database.

Checking the results can be done by adding together the values in `totalSales` and `totalCommission`. This "addition" is really accomplished by multiplying all the values together modulo p.

11.1.1 Adding Values

This example has a bit more overhead than usual. The software must use a consistent value of g and p every time it adds or multiplies a number. These are stored in one table, `protocolValues`, where they can be recovered by the method `fetchGP` every time the software restarts. The same values are used in Chapter 12, where similar values of $g^x \bmod p$ are stored away. In this chapter, the values are added together.

```
MD5 MD5Bean=new MD5();
java.util.Random ran;
DatabaseWrapper dw=new DatabaseWrapper();
```

```java
public void init(){
  dw.init();
  ran=new java.util.Random();
  initPS();
  fetchGP(protocolName);
 }

String protocolName="Alpha1";
BigInteger g,p;
BigInteger ceiling=BigInteger.valueOf(1000000000);

public void fetchGP(String protocol){
// The protocol is a string that maps to a pair.
 String findQuery="SELECT * FROM protocolValues WHERE name='";
 findQuery+=protocol+"'";;
   try{
      ResultSet rs=dw.executeQuery(findQuery);
      rs.next(); // get the first match.

      String gee=rs.getString("gee");
      String pea=rs.getString("pea");
      p=new BigInteger(pea);
      g=new BigInteger(gee);
   } catch (java.sql.SQLException e){
      System.out.println("SQL Exception:"+e);
   }
}
```

Here are a few `PreparedStatements` for accessing the database:

```java
PreparedStatement commissionSearch,productSearch;
PreparedStatement commissionInsert,productInsert;

public void initPS(){
   String q="SELECT * FROM commission WHERE name=?;";
   commissionSearch=dw.createPreparedStatement(q);

   q="SELECT * FROM products WHERE productLine=?;";
   productSearch=dw.createPreparedStatement(q);

   q="INSERT INTO commission SET name=?, totalCommission=?;";
   commissionInsert=dw.createPreparedStatement(q);

   q="INSERT INTO products SET productLine=?, totalSales=?;";
   productInsert=dw.createPreparedStatement(q);
}
```

This example includes two versions of the method `bigify` that adds a large random number greater than a constant `ceiling`. All values are assumed to be smaller than `ceiling` so adding this extra number prevents brute-force attacks without affecting consistency. The ceiling should be large enough to include all numbers up to the total. The size of the random number produced by `bigify` should be watched to avoid problems that may emerge if the values get larger than p. The sums are all limited by the size of $p - 1$.

This example also includes two ways to change the value in the database. The version of `ResultSet` in JDBC 2.0 includes several functions, like

updateString, that can update values in the row without changing other
columns. The other code without comments works with earlier versions of
the JDBC without these functions.

```java
public BigInteger bigify(int x){
    BigInteger extra=(new BigInteger(760, ran)).multiply(ceiling);
    return BigInteger.valueOf(x).add(extra);
}
public BigInteger bigify(){
  return (new BigInteger(760, ran)).multiply(ceiling);
 }


public void addToCommissions(String name, BigInteger amount){
  try{
    BigInteger newEntry=g.modPow(amount,p);
    commissionSearch.setString(1,name);
     ResultSet rs= commissionSearch.executeQuery();
    if (rs.next()){
        String com=rs.getString("totalCommission");
        BigInteger oldValue=new BigInteger(com);
        oldValue=oldValue.multiply(newEntry).mod(p);
        /*jdbc 2.0 use this:
          rs.updateString(2,oldValue.toString());
          rs.updateRow();
        if (!rs.rowUpdated()){
          System.out.println("Error with "+name+" amt:"+amount);
        }
        */

        String q="UPDATE commission SET totalCommission='"+oldValue;
        q=q+"' WHERE name='"+name+"';";
        dw.executeUpdate(q);

    } else {
       // add a new entry.
       commissionInsert.setString(1,name);
       commissionInsert.setString(2,newEntry.toString());
       commissionInsert.executeUpdate();
    }


} catch (SQLException e){
    System.out.println("SQLException:"+e);
}
}

public void addToSales(String name, BigInteger amount){
  try{
    BigInteger newEntry=g.modPow(amount,p);
    productSearch.setString(1,name);
     ResultSet rs= productSearch.executeQuery();
    if (rs.next()){
        String ss=rs.getString("totalSales");
        BigInteger oldValue=new BigInteger(ss);
        oldValue=oldValue.multiply(newEntry).mod(p);
```

```
        /*jdbc 2.0 use this:
           rs.updateString(2,oldValue.toString());
           rs.updateRow();
     if (!rs.rowUpdated()){
           System.out.println("Error: "+name+" amt:"+amount);
        }
        */

        String q="UPDATE products SET totalSales='"+oldValue;
        q=q+"' WHERE productLine='"+name+"';";
        dw.executeUpdate(q);

  } else {
        // add a new entry.
        productInsert.setString(1,name);
        productInsert.setString(2,newEntry.toString());
        productInsert.executeUpdate();
  }


} catch (SQLException e){
  System.out.println("SQLException:"+e);
}
}

public void reportSale(String sname, String pname, int amount){
    BigInteger b=bigify(amount);
    BigInteger com=b.divide(BigInteger.valueOf(10));
    b=com.multiply(BigInteger.valueOf(10)); // roundoff.
    addToSales(pname,b);
    addToCommissions(sname,com);
}
```

Here's a test case created by executing this code, which uses `reportSale`
to insert the results of recent sales by three people:

```
Commission c=new Commission();
c.init();

c.reportSale("Harrison Jones","cogs",1000);
c.reportSale("Candida Chile","springs",10000);

c.reportSale("Harrison Jones","springs",2000);
c.reportSale("Candida Chile","cogs",10000);
c.reportSale("Carrie Allen","springs",4000);
```

The tables looked like this after leaving off many of the digits:

name	totalCommission
Harrison Jones	45542114969245061494294451...
Candida Chile	84905148904002056375903375...
Carrie Allen	52057925313507721117851688...

productLine	totalSales
cogs	1317634539963832703065575586...
springs	7945050498623128610634633333...

11.1.2 Checking Things Out

If the values in `totalCommission` and `totalSales` are consistent, then everything should add up. That is, they should add up *after* multiplying them
modulo p. This code checks out the information by adding up the results in `totalCommission`, multiplying them by 10 (raising them to the 10th
power, modulo p), and then comparing the results by adding up the values
in `totalSales`. The `sumColumn` function adds up an arbitrary column from a
`ResultSet`, and then `testBalance` compares them. If the tables are accurate,
then everything will balance.

```
public BigInteger sumColumn(ResultSet rs, int column){
/// must be BigIntegers coded as strings.
  BigInteger t;
  try{
    BigInteger ans=BigInteger.valueOf(1);// g^0
    while (rs.next()){
      t=new BigInteger(rs.getString(column));
      ans=ans.multiply(t).mod(p);
    }
    return ans;
  } catch (SQLException e){
    System.out.println("SQLException:"+e);
  }
    return null;
}

public void testBalance(){
  try{
    ResultSet rs=dw.executeQuery("SELECT * FROM products;");
    BigInteger sales=sumColumn(rs,2);

    rs=dw.executeQuery("SELECT * FROM commission;");
    BigInteger com=sumColumn(rs,2);

    // multiply commissions by 10;
  com=com.modPow(BigInteger.valueOf(10),p);

    if (com.equals(sales)){
      System.out.println("Everything adds up.");
    } else {
      System.out.println("Something is inconsistent.");
    }
  } catch (Exception e){
    System.out.println("SQL Exception:"+e);
  }
```

11.2   Conclusions

Translucent data doesn't have to be static or completely inscrutable. The small accounting system here shows how tables of values can be kept and compared. The example adds numbers by multiplying the corresponding values in a discrete plane. The expression $x + y$ is equivalent to computing $g^x g^y \bmod p$.

Multiplication is also possible, but only if the value is not hidden by exponentiation. In the example, the size of the commissions is multiplied by 10 by raising it to the 10th power. It is not easy to multiply x by y when all you know about them is $g^x \bmod p$ and $g^y \bmod p$.

Multiplication is possible using RSA-like systems as one-way functions. In these, x is converted to $x^e \bmod pq$, where e is the public key, and p and q are two prime numbers. The variable d is the private key, which can be destroyed along with p and q to ensure that the function is truly one-way. Multiplying $x^e \bmod pq$ and $y^e \bmod pq$ produces $(xy)^e \bmod pq$, a trick that might be used to build an accounting system including multiplication. Unfortunately, there's no easy way to do addition with this construction.

This mechanism also offers a backdoor for decrypting the values if necessary. All the arithmetic can be completed by decrypting the values before the computation and then re-encrypting them afterwards, but that's a simple solution that requires knowledge of the private key. The principles of translucent data discourage the practice of letting anyone know this key.

11.2.1   Lessons

- Arithmetic modulo a prime number offers a way to do some mathematics in a complete translucent way. You can add up two lists of numbers and see whether they have the same totals.

- Multiplication modulo a pair of large prime numbers can also test to see whether two lists have the same product.

- These techniques are useful for accounting and other sensitive mathematical efforts, but they are also fragile. The algorithms cannot determine the difference without a brute-force search.

- Some brute-force searches are reasonable. Given $g^i \bmod p$, finding i may be as simple as testing small numbers.

- Many common numbers are not large enough to provide security. That is, testing all values less than 100,000 is simple for a standard personal computer. The solution is to add a large random value to each value.

Chapter 12

Tokens

In this world, there are translucent databases and then there are even more translucent databases. Some of the early chapters use one-way functions to hide the information used to search for data. If your name is x, then the database stores it under $h(x)$ to protect the value of your name. This is a perfectly reasonable solution that blocks people from figuring out your name from reading the database. But is it perfect?

There may be no truly secure system because an eavesdropper could find a way around this. Anyone listening in on the line between your computer and the database's server will be able to pick up $h(x)$. The intruder may not be able to learn the value of x from this but they will still know which value of $h(x)$ is linked to all your information. If the eavesdropper can see the database, then the eavesdropper can also look up all the past records stored under $h(x)$.

That is an more extreme vision of an attacker, and only the most serious collections of data will call for defending against these often mythical but occassionally real opponents. If you think your database falls into that category, then the solutions in this chapter may help you. This chapter explains how to use the public-key algorithms from Sections 4.2 and 10.1 to create a new token for recovering the data each time. Every time you return to the database, a different value will flow along the wire to recover your information.

This chapter inverts the digital signatures used in Chapter 10 to prove that a piece of data is authentic. In this chapter, a digital signature is the token to recover the information. The database asks the user to sign a different random value each time. If the signature is valid, then the person is assumed to have the right to see this data.

To put it mathematically, x is the private value, known only to the person, and the value of $h(x) = g^x \bmod p$ is used to search the database. To recover $h(x)$, you can provide either $h(x)$ itself or execute a digital signature in such a $g^x \bmod p$ is the public key. This chapter refers to this digital signature as a *token* because many digital currency systems use the same mechanism as a piece of digital cash.

The simple one-way functions in Chapters 3 and 5 produce simple tokens that are less secure, but easier to compute.

Controlling access to the database with tokens instead of $h(x)$ itself is more secure but also much less efficient. The search becomes much slower because the database must evaluate the digital signature for each row. It can't use the fast searching procedures that can work with the other algorithms. For that reason, we provide two methods for recovering data and suggest that the most secure be used in extreme cases.

12.1 Prescription Records

Imagine that you run a pharmacy holding records of who takes which drugs. Storing these records in a translucent database makes sense because the database allows you to place a low-security server under the counter of the drugstore. More secure, completely transparent records can be stored off-site where burglars, drug fiends and blackmail artists are less likely to find the information. The local machine can watch for dangerous drug interactions but remain secure even after a bad person steals the server with the intent of blackmailing the people taking socially stigmatized drugs.

Here's the SQL statement creating the table:

```
CREATE TABLE prescriptions1 (geex TEXT,drug CHAR(40), amount
INT,startDate TIMESTAMP, endDate TIMESTAMP);
```

The drug name goes in `drug`. The `startDate` and `endDate` fields hold the dates when the person should be starting and stopping the drug. The personal information is hidden behind a one-way function in `geex`. This is a `BigInteger` stored as text, partly to make this easier to debug and understand. A more robust version would store it as bytes to avoid reparsing it.

Light, seeking light, doth light of light beguile;
So ere you find where light in darkness lies,
Your light grows dark by losing of your eyes.
–William Shakespeare *Loves Labors Lost*

A translucent database makes sense for this application because the `startDate` and `endDate` values can be left in the clear and used to search for only the active prescriptions that can cause dangerous interactions.

Using the database calls for some added infrastructure. The implementations of public-key algorithms in Chapters 4 and 10 need a database of the public keys. In this example, the public keys ($g^x \bmod p$) are used to search the database, but other parts like g and p must still be stored in a publicly available location. That is, the part that is usually used as a public key is just used as a token to search the database.

Here's the code for initializing the Java class file used as a front end for the database:

```
MD5 MD5Bean=new MD5();
DatabaseWrapper dw=new DatabaseWrapper();
String protocolName="Alpha1";
BigInteger g,p;

public void init(){
  dw.init();
  initSQL();
  fetchGP(protocolName);
```

```
}

PreparedStatement ins;

public void initSQL(){
  String q="INSERT INTO prescriptions1 SET ";
  q=q+"geex=?,drug=?,amount=?,";
  q=q+"startDate=?,endDate=?;";
  ins=dw.createPreparedStatement(q);
}

public void createProtocol(String nm){
    MD5Bean.clear();
    MD5Bean.Update("Some randomness"+System.currentTimeMillis());
    MD5Bean.Update(nm);
    Random seed=new Random(MD5Bean.getMD5State().getStateInt(0));

    BigInteger p=new BigInteger(768, 5, seed );
    BigInteger g=new BigInteger(760, 5, seed );
  StringBuffer query=new StringBuffer();
  query.append("INSERT INTO protocolValues VALUES('");
  query.append(nm);
  query.append("','");
  query.append(g.toString());
  query.append("','");
  query.append(p.toString());
  query.append("');");


  System.out.println("query="+query);
  String q=query.toString();
  dw.executeQuery(q);
}

 public void fetchGP(String protocol){
// The protocol is a string that maps to a pair.
 String findQuery="SELECT * FROM protocolValues WHERE name='";
 findQuery+=protocol+"';";
   try{
     ResultSet rs=dw.executeQuery(findQuery);
     rs.next(); // get the first match.

     String gee=rs.getString("gee");
     String pea=rs.getString("pea");
       p=new BigInteger(pea);
        g=new BigInteger(gee);
   } catch (java.sql.SQLException e){
     System.out.println("SQL Exception:"+e);
   }
}
```

The functions createProtocol and fetchGP take care of a second table called protocolValues. This is just a link between a text string, the name, and a pair of values for g and p. It is created with this SQL statement:

```
CREATE TABLE protocolValues (name CHAR(40),gee TEXT, pea
TEXT);
```

This function uses only one pair which is stored under the name `Alpha1`. The database just makes it possible for both the clients and the server to share the same values of g and p. Other implementations may hard-code that information into the software, albeit with the usual general risks of obsolescence.

12.1.1   Inserting Records

The pharmacist inserts a new drug entry into `prescriptions1` with this code. The `generateX` function converts a passphrase into the private value of x, using an implementation of MD5 to hash the person's passphrase. The extra phrase, "Translucent Databases Rock!", just customizes the hash function.

```
public BigInteger generateX(String passphrase){
    MD5Bean.clear();
    MD5Bean.Update("Translucent Databases rock.");
    MD5Bean.Update(passphrase);
    byte[] hashedPass=MD5Bean.Final();
    return new BigInteger(hashedPass);
}

public void insertRecord(String passphrase,String drug,
                int amount,
                java.util.Date startDate,
                java.util.Date endDate){
  try{
    BigInteger x=generateX(passphrase);
    BigInteger gx=g.modPow(x,p);
    ins.setString(1,gx.toString());
    ins.setString(2,drug);
    ins.setInt(3,amount);
    ins.setTimestamp(4,new Timestamp(startDate.getTime()));
    ins.setTimestamp(5,new Timestamp(endDate.getTime()));
    ins.executeUpdate();
  } catch (SQLException e){
    System.out.println("SQL Exception:"+e);
  }
}
```

The code for `insertRecord` may include some extra code for testing for dependencies.

Here's a snapshot of the database with four records:

geex	drug	amount	startDate	endDate
442857631356...	Cipro	100	20020204000000	20020302000000
609964108595...	Cipro	100	20020204000000	20020302000000
609964108595...	Aflimax	100	20020304000000	20020328000000
109679242856...	Aflimax	100	20020204000000	20020214000000

The values of `geex` are truncated. The middle two records with $geex = 609964108595$ were created using the patient's name, "Harrison Jones", as the value of `passphrase`.

12.1.2 A Relatively Fast Mechanism for Retrieval

The fastest way to recover a person's records from `prescriptions1` is to grab the patient's passphrase, convert it into x using `generateX`, fetch the correct values of g and p, and then compute $g^x \bmod p$. Here is a set of methods that accomplish the computations:

```java
public void testGeeX(String passphrase){
  BigInteger x=generateX(passphrase);
  BigInteger gx=g.modPow(x,p);
  String q="SELECT * FROM prescriptions1 WHERE geex='";
  q=q+gx.toString();
  q=q+"';";

  java.util.Date start,end;
  String drug;
  int amount;
  try{
    ResultSet rs=dw.executeQuery(q);
    while (rs.next()){
      drug=rs.getString(2);
      amount=rs.getInt(3);
      start=new Date(rs.getTimestamp("startDate").getTime());
      end=new Date(rs.getTimestamp("endDate").getTime());
      System.out.print(drug+" ("+amount+")  St:");
      System.out.println(""+start+" End:"+end);
    }
  } catch (java.sql.SQLException e){
    System.out.println("SQL Exception:"+e);
  }
}
```

Of course, that fast method ships the value of $h(x) = g^x \bmod p$ in the clear so the database can `SELECT` the right rows using it. An eavesdropper could recover the value from this.

12.1.3 A More Secure Mechanism

A more secure mechanism is to treat the digital signature as a one-time key for unlocking the database. The rows with a public key that validates the digital signature are the ones returned by the search.

Here are the steps for the basic digital-signature scheme used in this section. You may want to use another one based on either the more popular RSA or the more standard DSS protocols.

1. The database generates a value of c. This will be the challenge. If the signature were to be applied to a document, then this would usually be the hash of the document, $h(document)$. In this case, c can be chosen at random by the database server. This guarantees that a different one will be used each time.

2. The client seeking the records generates a random value of w.

3. The client computes $r = cx + w$, where x is the private key.

4. The client offers r and $g^w \bmod p$ as the signature, based on c.

12.1.4 At the client

When the client computer wants to search the database, the client must generate a signature. This code takes a value of c computed by the server as a challenge and then returns the signature packed as a `String` for easy transport.

```
public String generateSignature(BigInteger c,
                                String passphrase){
  BigInteger x=generateX(passphrase);
  BigInteger w=new BigInteger(760,5,new Random());
  BigInteger r=w.add(c.multiply(x));
  BigInteger gw=g.modPow(w,p);

  BigInteger gx=g.modPow(x,p);

  return packSignature(c,r,gw);
}

public String packSignature(BigInteger c,
                            BigInteger r,
                            BigInteger gw){
  String ans= "c="+c.toString()+" r=";
  ans+=r.toString()+" gw="+gw.toString();
  return ans;
}
```

This signature does not reveal the value of x. It is different for every value of c presented to it, so it will be practically impossible for an eavesdropper to mimic its behavior without recovering x.

12.1.5 At the database

The database begins by generating a value of c at random. When the results come in, the database must evaluate the signatures and see whether they make sense.

Here's some code for checking the signature. The first version of `checkSignature` takes a string and unpacks the numbers so they can be understood by the second version.

```
 public boolean checkSignature(String sig, String geex){
// This strips away string packing.
   int pos=sig.indexOf("c=");
   int pos2=sig.indexOf(" ",pos);
   if (pos2<0){
     pos2=sig.length();
   }
   String cee=sig.substring(pos+2,pos2);

   pos=sig.indexOf("r=");
```

```
  pos2=sig.indexOf(" ",pos);
  if (pos2<0){
    pos2=sig.length();
  }
  String arr=sig.substring(pos+2,pos2);

  pos=sig.indexOf("gw=");
  pos2=sig.indexOf(" ",pos);
  if (pos2<0){
    pos2=sig.length();
  }
  String geew=sig.substring(pos+3,pos2);


  return checkSignature(geex,arr,geew,cee);
}


public boolean checkSignature(String geex, String arr,
                              String geew, String cee){
  BigInteger gx=new BigInteger(geex);
  BigInteger gw=new BigInteger(geew);
  BigInteger r=new BigInteger(arr);
  BigInteger c=new BigInteger(cee);



  BigInteger left=gx.modPow(c,p);
  left=left.multiply(gw).mod(p);
   BigInteger right=g.modPow(r,p);

  if (left.equals(right)){
    return true;
  }
  return false;
}
```

The signature-checking process compares the value of $g^r \bmod p$ and $(g^x \bmod p^x)^c \times (g^w \bmod p)$. If they are equal, the signature is valid.

Notice that this code leaves out an important step for the sake of clarity. It does not check to verify that the value of c sent out equals the value of c that returns. An attacker could replay an old request and reuse an old version of c.

The value of c doesn't even need to be packed into the signature in packSignature if the server can remember which version of c was passed to which process. Removing it from the transaction may speed it up.

12.1.6 Using transparency

Here's a quick example that shows how the server could check for other drugs in prescription1 on a particular date. It takes a signature and a date and then uses the built-in SQL functions to choose only the records describing prescriptions in use on the date.

```
public void fetchDrugs(String sig, java.util.Date dt){
```

```
  java.util.Date start,end;
  String drug;
  int amount;

try{
  java.sql.Timestamp ts=new java.sql.Timestamp(dt.getTime());
  lookup.setTimestamp(1,ts);
  lookup.setTimestamp(2,ts);
  ResultSet rs=lookup.executeQuery();

  while (rs.next()){
    String geex=rs.getString("geex");
    if (checkSignature(sig,geex)){
      drug=rs.getString(2);
      amount=rs.getInt(3);
      start=new Date(rs.getTimestamp("startDate").getTime());
      end=new Date(rs.getTimestamp("endDate").getTime());
    System.out.print(drug+" ("+amount+")  St:");
    System.out.println(""+start+" End:"+end);

    }
  }
} catch (java.sql.SQLException e){
    System.out.println("SQL Exception:"+e);
  }
}
```

12.1.7   Dealing with the Challenge

This example code uses this function to generate a challenge, c:

```
public BigInteger generateC(){
  return new BigInteger(750,5,new Random());
}
```

It works well, but there are other choices. The challenge can be generated by the client without interacting with the database. This cuts the number of steps in the protocol that must be carried out over a network. If the client creates the value of c, though, the server checking the signature must confirm that the value of c is different. A simple defense is to create a database of past signatures presented and then check to see whether the value of c is reused. Honest clients will always execute generateC before generateSignature. Dishonest ones won't.

Storing old values of c is clearly a trade-off. Is the extra work checking the old value better than adding an additional step to the protocol? It clearly depends on the cost of disk space, the number of queries generated each day and the network latency.

Another solution is to use a simple algorithm to generate a different value of c in such a way that both the client and server get the same answer. The simplest is to hash together the date and a password:

```
public BigInteger generateC(String passphrase){
  MD5Bean.clear();
  MD5Bean.Update(passphrase);
```

```
    Calendar now=Calendar.getInstance();
    String s=now.get(Calendar.MONTH)+":"+now.get(Calendar.DATE);
    s=s+":"+now.get(Calendar.YEAR);
    MD5Bean.Update(now.toString());
  byte[] hashedPass=MD5Bean.Final();
  return new BigInteger(hashedPass);
}
```

This value of c is good all day. After that day, it's worthless. The server will check the value of c presented and establish that it matches the correct value of c for this day. It's not possible to recover the value of the passphrase from the value of c so someone cannot take a signature and reuse it on another day.

12.2 Conclusions

Many earlier chapters in this book treat one-way functions as mathematical blenders for obscuring information. These are effective tools, but they may not provide enough solutions in all cases. This chapter expanded the notion by using the same functions in a similar way to produce values that are used only once. These solutions force the client to respond to a particular challenge that changes every time. An eavesdropper or casual attacker can't reuse the information provided by another.

These tricks are just another way to look at the idea of a digital signature. Instead of thinking of the signatures as guaranteeing a document, the person is asked to sign a new document to access data. The mathematics is the same, but the metaphor is flipped around.

12.2.1 Lessons

- This chapter also stores data in a table by obscuring x by storing $h(x) = g^x \bmod p$.

- Instead of forcing the client to ask for $h(x)$ by name, the database requires the client to create a digital signature, using the value of x as the private key.

- Eavesdroppers can't replay the process because a different digital signature is generated each time.

- To accomplish that, the value of $g^x \bmod p$ is stored as $h(x)$. This is usually considered the public key for Diffie-Hellman-like digital-signature schemes.

- The database provides a value of c that acts like a challenge.

- This value, c, can be determined randomly or based upon some shared algorithm. Hashing the date, for instance, produces a value of c that is good all day.

- Using a chain of hashes to produce c is another solution (See Chapter 6).

- Given c, the client creates a digital signature by producing $r = cx + w$ and $g^w \bmod p$.

- The client may also identify $g^x \bmod p$ to save the database some time.

- If the client doesn't identify $g^x \bmod p$, the signature must be compared against all entries.

- Schemes like these are less efficient because they call for checking multiple rows in the database, but they provide more security against eavesdroppers.

- Multiple tokens can be bundled together in much the same way that multiple credentials are bundled together in one big number. The algorithms from Section 8.4 can be retooled to work as tokens. The signature algorithms can sign parts of the entire certificate filled with data.

Chapter 13

Private Retrieval

Most of the algorithms in this book concentrate on protecting the information in the database from outside eyes. The more scrambled it is, the better. Sometimes the information in the database isn't what needs protection. Sometimes the questions people are asking should be cloaked.

Many algorithms in this book already protect the content of the questions. If someone requests all of the personal information available by asking for records where the $ID = h(name)$, then the name itself won't be revealed. Only the person asking the question will know it.

But there will be other cases– for example with public information or large public databases– where the data can't be scrambled. One of the classic examples of a case in which the data is public but the requests for data need to be cloaked lies in stock prices. Big investors often need to keep their plans secret from their brokers, if only to prevent their brokers from anticipating their transactions and betting that they will move the market. This action, called front-running, is illegal but difficult to catch and hard to prosecute. Savvy investors with big amounts to invest are careful about what they tell their brokers. In an ideal trading environment, they could get the price of a stock without revealing to the database which stock they wanted to see.

The algorithms in this chapter allow someone to look up information from a database without showing what information they need. That is often called *private information retrieval* or *oblivious transfer* by cryptography researchers. The terms describe problems that are closely related and, in a larger sense, practically the same.

There are two basic models of the problem. In one, the data is distributed between several servers that hold exact copies. A person sends a slightly different query to each server, combines the results and extracts the right information. The model works only if the servers don't communicate – something that seems unlikely in extreme situations but reasonable in some basic ones. For instance, no one can assume that the police won't use all of the information at their disposal if the case is serious, but minor crimes will often receive a small amount of attention.

That translucent alabaster of our memories.
–Marcel Proust
Remembrance of Things Past

167

The second model involves more computation, but it works with a single database. A single, more complex query is sent to a single database which sends back the information in such a way that only one record in the bunch can be recovered. These algorithms are popular with people who consider selling content online because they limit how much information is actually released from the database. While the database may package the results from n different records, the mathematics guarantees that the user can unpack only one of them.

These algorithms are limited in many ways, and all of them release some small amount of information if they are practical. The most secure versions may be theoretically compelling, but they're practically worthless. Researchers often compare their results against the *naive solution*, that is, just shipping the entire database to the user, who extracts the information in private. That would not expose anything to the database server, but it would be wasteful.

Practical solutions end up revealing some information by limiting the scope of the response. A request for stock quotes may only focus on a list of only 100 stocks in which 99 just distract attention from the one real request. Adding more distractions will increase the security but will also force every party to do more computation and move more information. Every user can determine the right amount of distraction for the user's needs.

13.1   Stock Prices From Multiple Sources

Imagine that you want to receive the price for a stock without unveiling your interest to your brokers or your brokers' computers. In the simplest case, you create a random list of n stocks, send this list off to one broker and ask that broker for the sum of the current prices of every stock. Then you add your stock to the list and send this list of $n + 1$ stocks to another broker with the same request. The price of the secret stock can be found by subtracting the first answer from the second.

Amos Beimel, Yuval Ishai and Tal Malkin describe an algorithm where some pre-processing by each server can cut the cost of answering queries [BIM00] while Yael Gertner, Shafi Goldwasser and Tal Malkin cut the server's work to a constant by calling for another class of random servers. [GGM98]

This solution can be generalized to work with m databases by asking the brokers to return the XOR ($\oplus$) of the stock prices instead of the simple sum. This approach works well with data that may not be strictly numerical. Computing the XOR of an array of bytes is easy to do, whether the array is a string or a collection of other bits. There are no issues with hwo the numbers are rounded off or represented.

Here's the algorithm:

1. Begin with m empty sets, $Q_1, Q_2, \ldots, Q_m$, representing the list of stocks to be sent to the m different brokers.

2. Repeat these steps n times to add n dummy stocks.

   (a) Choose a dummy stock.

(b) Choose a random even number, i, less than m.

(c) Add the dummy stock to i different queries chosen at random.

3. Choose a random odd number, i, less than m.

4. Add the stock of interest to i different query sets chosen at random.

5. Send the queries to the different brokers and ask them for the exclusive OR of the price of the stocks in their list. Call the results $F(Q_i)$.

6. When the results arrive, compute $F(Q_1) \oplus F(Q_2) \oplus F(Q_3) \ldots F(Q_m)$.

Mathematicians often consider XOR to be addition because it has the same properties. Section 7.1.2 describes some secret sharing solutions that use the same prinicples.

This algorithm works because $x \oplus x = 0$ and $x \oplus x$ is commutative. Adding in a stock an even number of times ensures that it is canceled out. Only stocks added an odd number of times will be left in the final total. If the query is computed correctly, then that will be the stock of interest.

If XOR is not available, it is possible to change this to add positive and negative weights to each stock. This may be useful if you're using some of the services that track the value of your portfolio. After choosing a random stock as a distracter, include 100 shares in one portfolio or query and subtract 100 shares in another by going short on the same stock.

Benny Chor, Niv Gilboa and Moni Naor describe a way to obfuscate a search for the information itself when the data is indexed by a keyword. [CGN97]

Obviously, the sizes of the queries and the number of them contribute to secrecy. There is a pretty straightforward trade-off between the number of stocks in the requests and the amount of secrecy. Many use information theory to analyze the algorithm and focus on the odds that a particular stock is the one in question. More dummy stocks decrease that the odds that a particular stock is *the one*. In a practical sense, there's little need to make the lists too large. There's a good chance that the stock of interest isn't on any particular Q_i so it could be any of the stocks in the database.

13.2 A Single-Server Example

Requiring the different databases to keep requests secret is a plausible request, but that requirement is hard to enforce. Detecting betrayal is difficult, if not practically impossible. Once your requests leave your computer, the brokers or eavesdroppers could be gathering the information and determining the target of your request.

A better solution uses only one database. A number of different algorithms can fetch information without revealing what's being requested, but all of them use more complicated mathematics.

Here is one algorithm that is close in spirit to the Diffie-Hellman algorithm used throughout this book. It relies upon the difficulty of computing the discrete logarithm for its strength. The algorithm essentially establishes two keys simultaneously in a way that only one will be valid. Only one party knows which one works. The other party encrypts two different chunks of data with the two keys, confident that the other party will be able to unscramble only one of them.

The basic algorithm establishes only two keys. That can be extended, though, by repeating it n times to obscure the selection of one item with $2^n - 1$ decoys. The process repeats the basic algorithm $\log_2 n$.

Here's the basic algorithm:

The digital signatures in Chapter 10 also use a challenge variable.

1. The user, or more properly the user's computer, and the database begin by agreeing on, C, a number that is often called a *challenge*. That value may be chosen by the database or established by computing the cryptographically secure hash of some common data, like the date and a person's login.

2. To make this description simpler, let D_0 be the item the user wants to retrieve and D_1 be the decoy. In practice, the user will choose the subscripts at random. Sometimes D_1 will be the data object of desire and D_0 will be the decoy.

3. The user creates a private key, x, and computes the public version, $K_0 = g^x \bmod p$, where p is a prime number and g is some generator for the group. The values of g and p are shared with the database, but the value of x is kept a secret.

4. The user computes $K_1 = \frac{C}{K_0} \bmod p$. That acts like a decoy. As long as the user has no control over the choice of C, the user won't be able to find a value of x' such that $K_1 = g^{x'} \bmod p$. This means that the user knows the corresponding private key for K_0 but not for K_1. The user will be able to decrypt one but not the other.

5. After the user presents K_0 and K_1, the database checks to see that $K_0 K_1 = C \bmod p$. If it does, then the database can be sure that the user could build the keys only by knowing one, but not both, of the private keys.

6. The database chooses two random values, r_0 and r_1, to act as keys.

7. The database computes $K_0^{r_0}$ and $K_1^{r_1}$.

8. The database scrambles D_0 with $h(K_0^{r_0})$ and D_1 with $h(K_1^{r_1})$ and sends these values to the user. The expression $h(x)$ is a cryptographically secure hash function.

9. The database also sends $g^{r_0} \bmod p$ and $g^{r_1} \bmod p$ to the user.

10. The user can unpack only one of these two because the user knows only one of the two private keys. In this case, the user knows x, which corresponds with K_0. The user can compute $(g^{r_0} \bmod p)^x \bmod p$, which happens to be equal to $K_0^{r_0}$. The user does not know any value of x' that can be used to compute $K_1^{r_1}$ from $g^{r_1} \bmod pm$ provided by the database.

11. The user unscrambles D_0, using $h((g^{r_0} \bmod p)^x \bmod p)$, and ignores D_1.

This algorithm allows the user to request two pieces of information from a database, D_0 and D_1, but unscramble only one of them, D_0.

13.2.1   Using More Decoys

Often one decoy is not enough. The algorithm is simple to extend to use more decoy and the real practical limit is the amount of data being requested. Using more decoys means that more data must be shipped to the user and that most of it will be discarded.

The best way to extend the algorithm for oblivious transfer is to think of it as providing part of the key for only half of the potential answers. In the first description, there were only two potential answers fetched from the database so the result was narrowed to one, D_0, after only one round. Think of that process as selecting the *zero half*.

The same algorithm could also choose the *one half* if the subscripts were flipped. To extend the algorithm, we'll present the database with a request for many items and then use the algorithm to cut the focus in half. Eventually, we'll be down to the one true request.

Let n be the smallest integer such that $2^n - 1$ is greater than or equal to the number of decoys needed. For the sake of simplicity, assume that we want $2^n - 1$ decoys to camouflage one real request. To do that this, we will repeat the oblivious-transfer algorithm n times.

Let $D_0 \ldots$ be the data items requested from the database. Let D_k be the real request. The others are decoys. The binary representation of k will guide the n different versions of the oblivious-transfer algorithm. For example, if $n = 4$ and $k = 0011$, then the user will ask for the *zero half*, the one that will unscramble D_0, the first two times it is used. The second two times, the user will choose the *one half*. Each iteration of the algorithm narrows the focus.

Being precise about this process is more a lesson in using nomenclature and choosing the right subscripts than a lesson in cryptography. Keeping the keys straight is a bit confusing, but the equations do little more than repeat the algorithm n times.

Here are some terms:

- Let $C_0, C_1, \ldots, C_{n-1}$ be the challenges chosen for each round.

- Let $K_{0,i}$ and $K_{1,i}$ be the two keys produced during round i.

- Let the private keys be $x_0, x_1, \ldots, x_{n-1}$.

- $C_i = K_{0,i} K_{1,i} \bmod p$ for all i.

- Only the user knows which values of x_i correspond to which public keys, $K_{0,i}$ or $K_{1,i}$. If the user is trying the narrow the search to the *zero half* during round i, then the user sets $K_{0,i} = g^{x_i} \bmod p$ and sets $K_{1,i} = \frac{C_i}{K_{0,i}}$.

If the user is after the *one half* during round i, then the user sets $K_{1,i} = g^{x_i} \mod p$.

- The database chooses random values $r_{0,i}$ and $r_{1,i}$ for rounds $0, 1, \ldots, n-1$.

- Let $m(b, i) = H(K_{b,i}^{r_{b,i}})$. These will be the parts of the key used to scramble the data.

- $M(j)$ be computed by XOR'ing together the values of $m(b, i)$ computed from the binary representation of j. So if $j = 0011$, then $M(0011) = m(0,0) \oplus m(0,1) \oplus m(1,2) \oplus m(1,3)$.

- Data item D_j is scrambled with the key $M(j)$.

That's a long list of definitions. The most important point is that the user can compute only one value of $M(j)$, the one that corresponds to the values of $x_0, x_1, x_2 \ldots x_{n-1}$. All of the others are inscrutable.

It should be noted that this algorithm does not need to be repeated n times. Each iteration cuts the size of the answers in half. It's possible to begin with 256 requests, run the algorithm four times and reduce the size to 16 real requests. If you have more than one request, then this can be a more efficient solution.

13.3   A Patent Example

Imagine that you're a new inventor who wants to explore the idea of getting a patent, a process that involves reading plenty of past patents to see if your invention is truly novel. That means making many trips to the patent database. If someone at the patent office is watching your movements, that person may be able to find out enough to beat you to the punch.

Here's Java code for generating a set of keys for scrambling the patent requests. The inventor requests 2^n patents, $D_0, D_1, \ldots D_{n-1}$, and the patent database scrambles them with keys $M(0), M(1), \ldots, M(n-1)$. This algorithm is useful because many patent databases support themselves by charging by the copy. The database's administrators can charge the inventor using this algorithm for only one copy, although 2^n are actually delivered in scrambled form. Only one of the 2^n can actually be decoded.

The implementation relies heavily on Java's `BigInteger` package. That package creates random arrays of `BigIntegers`, a process used to create the private keys, $\{x_0, x_1, \ldots, x_{n-1}\}$; the challenges, $\{C_0, C_1, \ldots, C_{n-1}\}$; and the random values, $\{r_{0,0}, r_{1,0}, r_{0,1}, r_{1,1}\}$.

```
public BigInteger[] generateBigArray(int n){
  BigInteger[] ans=new BigInteger[n];
  for (int i=0;i<n;i++){
    ans[i]=new BigInteger(bitSize,ran).mod(p);
  }
```

```
    return ans;
}

public BigInteger[][] generateBigArray(int n,int m){
  BigInteger[][] ans=new BigInteger[n][m];
  for (int i=0;i<n;i++){
    for (int j=0;j<m;j++) {
      ans[i][j]=new BigInteger(bitSize,ran).mod(p);
    }
  }
  return ans;
}
```

The public keys created by the user come from this code. It takes the private key, the challenges and the index of the real request, k.

```
public boolean bitTest(int i, int bit){
  return ((i & (1 << bit))!=0);
}
public BigInteger[][] generatePublicKeys(BigInteger[] challenges,
                                         BigInteger[] privates,
                                         int k, int n){
    BigInteger[][] ans=new BigInteger[2][n];
    for (int i=0;i<n;i++){
      if (bitTest(k,i)){
        ans[0][i]=g.modPow(privates[i],p);
        ans[1][i]=challenges[i].multiply(ans[0][i].modInverse(p));
      } else {
        ans[1][i]=g.modPow(privates[i],p);
        ans[0][i]=challenges[i].multiply(ans[1][i].modInverse(p));
      }
    }
    return ans;
}
```

The user takes this array produced by generatePublicKeys and hands it over to the database. The values of the private keys and k are kept secret.

The database generates random values of r with the function generateBigArray(n,2) and uses this code to do all of the exponentiation.

```
public BigInteger[][] powerCompose(BigInteger[][] value,
                                   BigInteger[][] exponents,
                                   int n,int m){
  BigInteger[][] ans=new BigInteger[n][m];
  for (int i=0;i<n;i++){
    for (int j=0;j<m;j++) {
      ans[i][j]=value[i][j].modPow(exponents[i][j],p);
    }
  }
  return ans;
}
```

The result can be used to compute the values of $M(i)$. This routine uses a slightly different process. Instead of XOR'ing together the results from hashing all the values individually, all the results are just hashed together in one big block. The 16 byte array is the key for k. The database would repeat this 2^n times.

```
public byte[] composeKeys(BigInteger[][] keys,int k,int n){
  MD5Bean.clear();
  for (int i=0;i<n;i++){
    if (bitTest(k,i)){
        MD5Bean.Update(keys[0][i].toString());
      } else {
        MD5Bean.Update(keys[1][i].toString());
    }
  }
  return MD5Bean.Final();
}
```

This code can be used to find the values of $M(k)$. A one-dimensional version of powerCompose does the work of combining the values for the user.

13.4   Conclusions

Cloaking the target of your request using the algorithms in this chapter is often useful when looking up information in large public databases. The information itself may not be sensitive enough to keep scrambled, but there may be plenty of value in the metadata about who wants to know what.

Many other algorithms in this book provide some level of protection by scrambling the information itself. If only the person retrieving the information knows what it means, an eavesdropper can't tell much about the metadata. But there are other cases in which the algorithms in this chapter may be used independent of the other solutions.

13.4.1   Lessons

- The simplest solution is to request different collections of data from different sources. If the sources don't communicate, that can be quite secure. For instance, asking one database for $A \oplus B \oplus C \oplus D$ and another for $B \oplus C \oplus D$ effectively reveals A.

- Approaching one database with an oblivious-transfer algorithm eliminates the need to trust multiple databases to remain mum. These algorithms send a request for two items. The database responds and scrambles them so only one of the two can be decoded. The client makes the choice, but the database doesn't know which was unscrambled.

- The oblivious-transfer algorithm can be repeated $\log_2 n$ times to let someone request $n - 1$ decoys to cloak one real request.

Appendix A

Further Reading

This book is meant to be a concise exploration of how to mix databases and cryptography. Both topics are deep, complicated and rich subjects, filled with many nuances and difficult points. If you're thinking of using these ideas in production systems, please consider reading further in these areas.

General Cryptography The *Handbook of Applied Cryptography* by Alfred Menezes, Paul von Oorschot and Scott Vanstone [MvV97] is an excellent general reference for many basic and advanced topics. The book contains a relatively deep discussion of practical issues for implementing the algorithms. Bruce Schneier's *Applied Cryptography* [Sch95] is another excellent reference with a broader scope.

Databases There are hundreds of books about databases, and it would be difficult to mention all of them. There are many different and subtle points that affect the speed and the accuracy of databases. This book avoids many of these issues by treating data as a broad abstraction defined by SQL. Talented database administrators will want to pay careful attention to how and why to make certain choices when using the techniques in production environments.

Steganography The science of hiding information is known as steganography. In the most abstract sense, the technology opens up another channel for carrying extra information inside a traditional channel. Music publishers, for instance, want to embed data about copyright and ownership in the noise of the music. Photographers want to create a digital watermark that carries a copyright notice and information about reproduction rights. Some researchers want to use that channel to update software packages. A digital copy of an X-ray might carry some comments from a doctor. The additional channel holds the data without breaking the previous generation of software.

Steganography is a powerful technique to use with translucent databases. If extra information can be hidden by forming it into a traditional form, then all of the traditional tools for a database can still act upon it.

Disappearing Cryptography is one book I wrote about the subject. [Way96, Way02] Ingemar J. Cox, Matthew L. Miller, and Jeffrey A. Bloom wrote *Digital Watermarking*, an excellent treatment of the subfield. [CMB01] *Information Hiding : Steganography and Watermarking – Attacks and Countermeasures* by Neil F. Johnson, Zoran Duric, and Sushil Jajodia focuses on hiding information in sound and image files and also detecting the presence of hidden information. [JDJ01]

Subliminal Channels This technique packs an additional message into a digital signature. Gus Simmons found that many of the most common digital signature algorithms can carry some additional bits with the value of the signature. [Sim84, Sim85, Sim86, Sim93, Sim94] Some of the common signature-only algorithms like the El Gamal signature scheme, [ElG85] or the Digital Signature Algorithm, [??93] depend upon a seemingly random number. If this value isn't chosen completely at random, the values bundled into the digital signature can carry extra information. That may be used in a translucent database for any number of purposes, including providing extra detail (Chapter 9), providing extra authentication (Chapter 10) or just carrying extra information away from prying eyes.

Encryption Toolkits Several good toolkits for encrypting data can be found on the Internet. The OpenSSL project, for instance, offers a sophisticated modern version of the original SSLeay package created by Eric Young and Tim Hudson. It can be downloaded from `www.openssl.org/`. The GNU Project (`www.gnu.org`) also includes an excellent encryption tool, GNU Privacy Guard, which can be downloaded from `www.gnupg.org`. A number of commercial packages are available from companies like RSA Data Security, Baltimore Technologies and Phaos.

Bibliography

[??93]   ?? A guide to understanding covert channel analysis of trusted systems. Technical Report TG-030, NCSC, November 1993.

[Ber00]   Alex Berenson. On hair-trigger wall street, a stock plunges on fake news. *New York Times*, August 2000.

[BIM00]   Amos Beimel, Yuval Ishai, and Tal Malkin. Reducing the servers computation in private information retrieval: PIR with preprocessing. In *CRYPTO 2000*, pages 55–73, 2000.

[BR99]   Mihir Bellare and Ronald L. Rivest. Translucent cryptography — an alternative to key escrow, and its implementation via fractional oblivious transfer. *Journal of Cryptology: the journal of the International Association for Cryptologic Research*, 12(2):117–139, 1999.

[Bra95]   Stefan A. Brands. *Rethinking Publike Key Infrastructure and Digital Certificates– Building in Privacy*. PhD thesis, Centrum voor Wiskunde en Informatica, Amsterdam, 1995.

[Bri00]   Ted Bridis. Microsoft acknowledges its engineers placed security flaw in some software. *Wall Street Journal*, April 2000.

[CA01]   Christopher Cooper and Chris Adams. Who gave the hijackers visas? a tough job gets tougher. *Wall Street Journal*, November 2001.

[CGN97]   Benny Chor, Niv Gilboa, and Moni Naor. Private information retrieval by keywords. Technical Report TR CS0917, Department of Computer Science, Technion, 1997.

[CMB01]   Ingemar J. Cox, Matthew L. Miller, and Jeffrey A. Bloom. *Digital Watermarking*. Morgan Kaufman, San Fransisco, CA, 2001.

[DH76a]   W. Diffie and M.E. Hellman. Multiuser cryptographic techniques. In *Proceedings of AFIPS National Computer Conference*, 1976.

[DH76b]   W. Diffie and M.E. Hellman. New directions in cryptography. *IEEE Transactions on Information Theory*, IT-22(6), Nov 1976.

[DH77]   W. Diffie and M.E. Hellman. Exhaustive cryptanalysis of the nbs data encryption standard. *Computer*, 10(6), Jun 1977.

[ElG85]   T. ElGamal. A public-key cryptosystem and a signature scheme based on discrete logarithms. In *Advances in Cryptology: Proceedings of CRYPTO 84*. Springer-Verlag, 1985.

[Elr01]   M.L. Elrich. Cops tap database to harass, intimidate: Misuse among police frequent, say some, but punishments rare. *Detroit Free Press*, July 2001.

[FK89]   David C. Feldmeier and Philip R. Karn. UNIX password security - ten years later. In *CRYPTO*, pages 44–63, 1989.

[Fou98]   Electronic Frontier Foundation. *Cracking DES:Secrets of Encryption Research, Wiretap Politics & Chip Design*. O'Reilly, Sebastopol, California, June 1998.

[GGM98] Yael Gertner, Shafi Goldwasser, and Tal Malkin. A random server model for private information retrieval (or information theoretic PIR avoiding database replication. In M. Luby, J. Rolim, and M. Serna editors, editors, *RANDOM '98, 2nd International Workshop on Randomization and Approximation Techniques in Computer Science*, volume 1518 of Lecture Notes in Computer Science, pages 200–217. Springer-Verlag, 1998.

[Jac01] Tom Jackmon. Dmv clerk is target of bribe: $10,000 allegedly paid for learner's permits issued to teens. *Washington Post*, November 2001.

[JDJ01] Neil F. Johnson, Zoran Duric, and Sushil Jajodia. *Information Hiding: Steganography and Watermarking - Attacks and Countermeasures (Advances in Information Security, Volume 1)*. Kluwer Academic Publishers, February 2001.

[Lem00] Robert Lemos. Insider threat to faa systems? new report says federal aviation administration is still not protecting its systems against personnel with inadequate security clearance. *Ziff-Davis Network*, June 2000.

[Man95] Mark Manasse. The millicent protocols for electronic commerce. In *1st USENIX workshop on Electronic Commerce*, July 1995.

[Man96] Udi Manber. A simple scheme to make passwords based on one-way functions much harder to crack, 1996.

[McC01] Declan McCullagh. 'secure' u.s. site wasn't very. *Wired News*, July 2001.

[MT79] Robert Morris and Ken Thompson. Password security: A case history. *CACM*, 22(11):594–597, 1979.

[Mur00] Dean E. Murphy. Irresistible lure of subways keeps landing impostor in jail. *New York Times*, August 2000.

[MvV97] Alfred J. Menezes, Paul C. van Oorschot, and Scott A. Vanstone. *Handbook of Applied Cryptography*. CRC Press, New York, 1997.

[OOM99] Aleksander Ohrn and Lucila Ohno-Machado. Using boolean reasoning to anonymize databases. *Artificial Intelligence in Medicine*, 15(3):235–254, 1999.

[Ras01] William K. Rashbaum. Brooklyn officers accused as brazen robbers. *New York Times*, January 2001.

[Riv98] Ron Rivest. Chaffing and winnowing: Confidentiality without encryption. *CryptoBytes (RSA Laboratories)*, 4(1):12–17, summer 1998.

[RRA78] Adi Shamir Ron Rivest and Len Adleman. A method for obtaining digital signatures and public-key cryptosystems. *Communications of the ACM*, 21(11), 1978.

[Sch95] Bruce Schneier. *Applied Cryptography: Protocols, Algorithms, and Source Code in C*. John Wiley and Sons, 2 edition, 1995.

[Sha79] Adi Shamir. How to share a secret. *Communications of the ACM*, 22(11):612–613, 1979.

[Sim84] G.J. Simmons. The prisoner's problem and the subliminal channel. In *Advances in Cryptology: Proceedings of CRYPTO '83*. Plenum Press, 1984.

[Sim85] G.J. Simmons. The subliminal channel and digital signatures. In *Advances in Cryptology: Proceedings of EUROCRYPT 84*. Springer-Verlag, 1985.

[Sim86] G.J. Simmons. A secure subliminal channel (?). In *Advances in Cryptology–CRYPTO '85 Proceedings*. Springer-Verlag, 1986.

[Sim93] G.J. Simmons. The subliminal channels of the U.S. Digital Signature Algorithm (DSA). In *Proceedings of the Third Symposium on: State and Progress of Research in Cryptography*, Fondazone Ugo Bordoni, Rome, 1993.

[Sim94] G.J. Simmons. Subliminal communication is easy using the DSA. In *Advances in Cryptology–EUROCRYPT '93 Proceedings*. Springer-Verlag, 1994.

[SS00] P. Samarati and L. Sweeney. Protecting privacy when disclosing information: k-anonymity and its enforcement through generalization and suppression(unpublished). Technical report, Carnegie-Mellon University, 2000.

[Swe96]   Latanya Sweeney. Replacing personally identifying information in medical records, the scrub system. *Journal of the American Medical Informatics Association*, pages 333–337, 1996.

[Swe97]   Latanya Sweeney. Guaranteeing anonymity when sharing medical data, the datafly system. *Journal of the American Medical Informatics Association*, 1997.

[Syv98]   Syverson. Weakly secret bit commitment: Applications to lotteries and fair exchange. In *PCSFW: Proceedings of The 11th Computer Security Foundations Workshop*. IEEE Computer Society Press, 1998.

[TPM01]   Tom Topousis, Rocco Parascandola, and Erika Martinez. Cops: Subway clerk stole $327,000. *New York Post*, 2001.

[unk00a] unknown. Ex-worker found guilty of computer sabotage. *Reuters*, May 2000.

[unk00b] unknown. Intel workers indicted for alleged software piracy. *Reuters*, May 2000.

[Vog00]   Steve Vogel. A 'major' misuse of weapons alleged. *Washington Post*, August 2000.

[Way92]   Peter C. Wayner. Content-addressable search engines and DES-like systems. In *Advances in Cryptology: CRYPTO '92 Lecture Notes in Computer Science, volume 740*, pages 575–586, New York, 1992. Springer-Verlag.

[Way96]   Peter Wayner. *Disappearing Cryptography*. AP Professional, Chestnut Hill, MA, 1996.

[Way02]   Peter Wayner. *Disappearing Cryptography, 2nd Edition*. Morgan Kaufman, San Fransisco, CA, 2002.

Index